Service Mining

Service Mining

Framework and Application

Wei-Lun Chang

First published in 2014 by
Business Expert Press, LLC
222 East 46th Street, New York, NY 10017
www.businessexpertpress.com

ISBN-13: 978-1-60649-574-2 (paperback)
ISBN-13: 978-1-60649-575-9 (e-book)

Business Expert Press Quantitative Approaches to Decision Making
Collection

Collection ISSN: 2163-9515 (print)
Collection ISSN: 2163-9582 (electronic)

Cover and interior design by Exeter Premedia Services Private Ltd.,
Chennai, India

First edition: 2014

10 9 8 7 6 5 4 3 2 1

Printed in the United States of America.

Abstract

The shifting focus of service from the 1980s to 2000s has proved that IT not only lowers the cost of service but creates avenues to enhance revenue through service. In particular, companies increase revenue through IT-based services. The new type of service, e-service, has several features such as being mobile, flexible, interactive, and interchangeable. Additionally, e-services have much to offer in terms of overcoming obstacles faced by a traditional services industry. The concept of service science, which was proposed by IBM, combines several issues into traditional service management, such as the disciplines of technology and engineering. While service science provides an avenue for future service researches, the specific research areas from the IT perspective still needs to be elaborated. This book introduces a novel concept, service mining, to address several research areas from the viewpoints of technology, model, management, and application. Service mining is defined as "a systematical process including service discovery, experience, recovery, and retention to discover unique patterns and exceptional values within the existing services." The goal of service mining is similar to data mining, text mining, or web mining—it aims to "detect something new" from the service pool. The major difference is the feature of service is quite distinct in its mining target such as data or text. In other words, service is a process of value co-creation and difference in the perception of various customers. In the concept of service mining, the target is not only the traditional services but also IT-based services. Service mining is a branch under the big umbrella of service science. The goals of this book are to devise various concepts of service mining and to identify different possible applications. The contribution is to furnish a roadmap of service mining to researchers, managers, and marketers in service sectors.

Keywords

service mining, service cooperation, service branding, service idealism, pricing, value network

Contents

Introduction

Service industry currently dominates the contribution to GDP for most countries. The focus has shifted from manufacturing to service. Many companies attempted to explore the services sector and as a result many innovative services emerged in the past decade. Therefore, delving deeper to look at services is important to companies. Traditional service marketing and service science attempted to help companies understand what customers think and how companies dealt with problems. However, a holistic framework and viewpoint to explore services differently is needed. Service mining provides a different perspective into the services industry. Professionals and practitioners also need various mindsets to investigate and analyze the evidence from services. According to the concept of service science, certain areas are involved such as economics, management, computer science, and engineering. This book provides a novel concept to combine the areas of social science and computer science in services. Service mining is a holistic concept covering a service's lifecycle from design, experience, recover to retain. Traditionally, the value of mining is to discover unknown and potential patterns from big data. Service mining focuses on the amount of data generated from the value co-creation process and features of services. The goal of service mining is to analyze any step in the service's lifecycle and help enterprises reexamine each one. Companies can also utilize appropriate marketing or management methods to adjust biases and revise the errors of services. This book covers various issues of service mining in eight chapters. Chapter 1 introduces the concept and framework of service mining, which may give readers a holistic view of service mining. In academics or practice, service mining has many opportunities for further investigation. Chapter 2 introduces a new perspective to the discussion of customer value on electronic services. Different from a conventional accounting perspective, a new customer value model is needed to understand what the value of a customer is again. Chapter 3 discusses the pricing model for electronic services. Compared to existing pricing methods, customer-perceived value-based pricing model is the new trend in service pricing. Particularly, service is different from customers and companies can use dynamic pricing concept to earn more profit based on customer perceptions. Chapter 4 discusses the importance of service cooperation. Services can cooperate based on the same value and vision. A new perspective from a customer's viewpoint is proposed in this chapter. Chapter 5 introduces the prediction of electronic services in customer relationship management. Although customer behavior is difficult to capture and predict, the pattern still exists and is valuable for further investigation. Chapter 6 uses a new notion called system dynamics to look at the service failure and recovery. System dynamics provides a way to simulate the policy in a long-term period. Companies can track and understand what would occur if they adjust services and benefit in the long run. Chapter 7 mentions the issue of service branding. In this chapter, the customers apparel is the key factor to build the service brand image. Traditionally, a brand image is delivered by a company based on vision and mission. Service mining provides a different perspective to explore what a service brand looks like based on customer viewpoint. Chapter 8 provides a new mindset when looking for the ideal services, which is service idealism. In this chapter, customer viewpoint is the basis to construct the elements of an ideal service. Readers can have a comprehensive knowledge and the basic framework of service mining. In this book, the selected areas of service mining come from various perspectives, which are also the potential and hot topics by far. Such areas enfold different stakeholders for service mining, including customers (Chapters 2, 3, and 5) as well as service providers (Chapters 3, 4, 5, 6, 7, and 8). Except for the phase of design in the service lifecycle, Chapters 2 to 8 synthesizes the concepts of four phases. For example, discovery (Chapters 2, 5, and 8), experience (Chapters 3, 4, 6, and 8), recovery (Chapter 6), retention/loyalty (Chapter 5). By examining different issues, readers can understand the potential development of service mining and obtain new applications in service industry. With this book, readers can have a new mindset to experience services. Companies can also reconsider the problems in services by matching the service lifecycle. Different mining methods can also be used to diagnose and analyze the real problems in design, experience, and failure. Surely, good services will also be discovered to retain for more profit. In summary, this book not only provides a new mindset for researchers but also furnishes certain applications for firms to reexamine the services. Professionals and practitioners can look into services from different viewpoints and use different methods for analysis based on the concept of service mining. Additionally, new issues may be explored, based on the provided topics and applications, to construct a more comprehensive skeleton of service mining in the future.

CHAPTER 1

Framework and Opportunities of Service Mining

The evolution of services from the 1980s to 2000s has proved that information technology (IT) not only lowers the cost of service but also creates avenues to enhance revenue through services.[1] Companies now increase their revenue through IT-based services and they face marketing challenges for e-service through different channels.[2] The new type of services (IT-enabled) and e-services have several features, such as being mobile, flexible, interactive, and interchangeable.[3] E-services provide a viable alternative for overcoming obstacles faced by traditional services industry. The essential change in the way services are delivered also forces companies to innovate, design, and deliver services through new channels.

Service science is a novel concept that offers a new paradigm for the future of service industry. The concept of service science was proposed by IBM, which solves several issues in traditional service management using technology and engineering.[4] For example, the focus of call centers has been shifted from collaborate to automate with IT assistance over the last decades (Figure 1.1). The paradigm of service has undergone a transformation from the traditional services industry to an IT-based services industry. FedEx presents an excellent example of a switch to e-services, which includes self-service, customization, search engine, flexibility, and automatic response.[5] Google is another great example of a global enterprise providing IT-based services (i.e., e-services) in the new paradigm.[6] Information technology helps automate services to allow more interactions between service providers and customers. Such interactions result in increasing the significance of value co-creation for both sides.

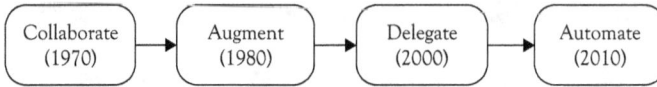

Collaborate (1970) → Augment (1980) → Delegate (2000) → Automate (2010)

Figure 1.1 **Example of changes of service paradigm**

Source: Spohrer and Maglio (2008).

The history of mining techniques starts from 1990s. The first concept to appear was data mining, which aims to extract information from a dataset and transform it into an understandable structure for future use. After data mining, researchers and practitioners extended to text and web mining. Text mining, the second mining concept to be described, aims to derive patterns in a structured text and interpret the output accordingly. The third concept, web mining, discovers useful and previous unknown information from web data. While the mining techniques still exist, a new paradigm of mining from services perspective needs to be explored and investigated.

The concept of service science encompasses several areas such as design, marketing, computer science, system engineering, economics and law, and operations. This book provides perspectives from computer science and marketing as a holistic viewpoint by injecting traditional data mining mindset. Hence, this book proposes a novel concept, service mining, to cover several aspects from the viewpoints of technology, model, management, and application. Service mining is defined as "a systematical process including service discovery, service experience, service recovery and service retention to discover unique patterns and exceptional values within the existing services." The goal of service mining, which is similar to data mining, text mining, or web mining, is to "detect and analyze something new (unknown, potential, and useful patterns)" from services (Table 1.1). The major difference is the "feature of service," which is quite distinct from mining targets such as data or text. Data and text are generated passively but service is a collaborative activity. Service is a process of value co-creation and differentiation using various perceptions of the customer.

According to the roadmap of service science, management, and engineering (SSME), service mining emphasizes on "systems that focus on flows of things" and "systems that support people's activities." Service mining focuses on stakeholders (e.g., providers and customers) and

Table 1.1 Comparison of different mining approaches

Type of mining	Idea	Mining target
Data mining	Extract information from a data set and transform it into an understandable structure	Data
Text mining	Derive patterns with structured text and interpret the output	Structured text
Web mining	Discovers useful and previous unknown information from web data	Structured web data
Service mining	Detect and analyze something new (unknown, potential, and useful patterns) from services	Service (features) and behavioral data (co-created by providers and customers)

resources (e.g., people, technology, and information). Service mining assists in observing and analyzing the behaviors of stakeholders as well as in resources allocation. This book expects to add the value of service mining to business and society, particularly, contributing to service industry.

Service mining focuses on two types of mining targets: feature of service and the combined behavioral data of providers and customers. Feature of service means the various elements of service such as service alliance, cooperation, and competition from the provider perspective. Behavioral data is most likely the same as data mining in the traditional sense. However, the difference is service data takes into account more interactive behavior whereas traditional mining data focuses on fixed behavior. For example, customers exhibit different attitude or behavior toward different service providers, resulting in dynamic service data. Service mining not only covers the area of traditional services but also IT-based services. Under the big umbrella of service science, service mining is considered as a new branch and extension of data mining application.

Service Mining Basis: Service Lifecycle

Figure 1.2 demonstrates a process of service lifecycle, including design, experience, recovery, and retention/loyalty. Service lifecycle synthesizes and derives the idea from service blueprinting.[7] Service design and discovery is more technology-oriented and service recovery and

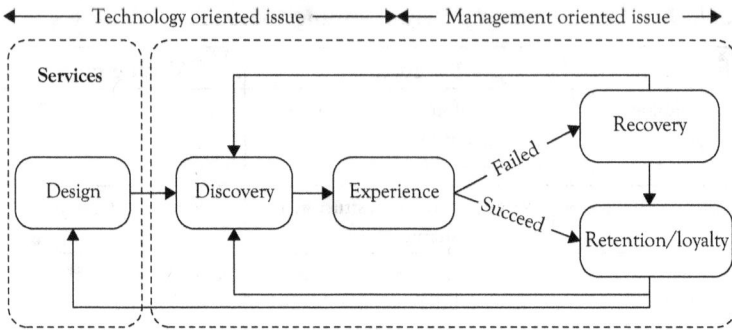

Figure 1.2 Service lifecycle

retention/loyalty are more management oriented. Particularly, service experience includes both these orientations:

- **Service design**
  The purpose of this phase is to use design thinking concept to come up with innovative services. Experts from design, technology, management, and art areas can work together to simulate what how services need to be defined. Service design is the beginning phase of service lifecycle and necessary for following processes.
- **Service discovery**
  The purpose of this phase is to discover potential services for customers from existing services. Service discovery also aims to explore service products in the market. Traditionally, web service is a hot topic in this category. However, web service is designed for machine-to-machine cooperation that mainly relies on technology. Other than web services, traditional services or IT-enabled services are the main focus in this phase.
- **Service experience**
  This phase facilitates the engineering and delivery of service. Service experience emphasizes on "how to provide appropriate services to right customers" by collaboration. The reason to use "appropriate" is that service is different for different customers by perception. It is difficult to justify "right services" in general. The ultimate goal is to collaborate with customers to co-create service value.

- **Service recovery**

  In this phase, service recovery mostly focuses on how to recover services when a service fails. Customers may be dissatisfied with companies if the recovery process does not happen on time. Customer complaints also occur at this moment. The goal is to provide in-time services to recover failure and adjust the mistakes made. Generally, service recovery is extremely important for enterprises to maintain customer satisfaction and loyalty.

- **Service retention and loyalty**

  The last phase of service lifecycle is service retention and loyalty. Service retention/loyalty specifies retaining appropriate services for customers. Companies may provide many services; however, only a few services are appropriate and useful to customers. The goal of this phase is to recognize and retain helpful and proper services that may create profits for firms.

Service mining covers the whole service lifecycle. Technology can be used to assist any phase in the lifecycle. Service retention and loyalty provide the most valuable information in service lifecycle. This information will be passed to the service design phase to help companies design better services. Taking an example of a city tour service for a customer in Chicago, there are certain designed services (e.g., city segway tour, speedboat, tastebud food tour, etc.). Customers have different preferences; therefore, discovering appropriate services that suit them is extremely important. Customer feedback and perception may be generated during the service experience. Spontaneous and instant responses can help adjust services for the tour guide. In addition, many companies ask customers to provide positive feedback and credit on TripAdvisor (e.g., city segway tour and tastebud food tour). After experiencing services, customers may rate the service as a success or a failure. If services failed, recovery is significant to reduce negative customer perception. The company can revise the service instantly. For example, a customer complained about why the raincoat needs $1 because the tour already charged $70, the city segway company instantly cancelled the policy and started to provide free raincoat and bottles of water. If services succeeded, keeping retention and loyalty of services are needed. Some companies e-mailed coupons for next-time purchase or experience to keep customers (e.g., California Pizza Kitchen).

The concept of service lifecycle covers exploratory service to service maintenance, which also provides the opportunities to people in both IT and management to get involved in service mining.

A Conceptual Framework of Service Mining

In addition to service lifecycle, a conceptual framework for service mining is also needed (Figure 1.3). From bottom to top, service mining covers five elements: infrastructure, technology, modeling, marketing/management, and application:

- **Infrastructure**
  Infrastructure indicates the basic elements and covers the necessary software and hardware in the service lifecycle. The software and hardware can be tangible or intangible assets. Service mining is based on services furnished by required software and hardware (IT infrastructure).
- **Technology**
  Technology indicates the techniques used to analyze for services in service mining, such as artificial intelligence or computer science. Examples of artificial intelligence include genetic algorithm, neural network, reinforcement learning,

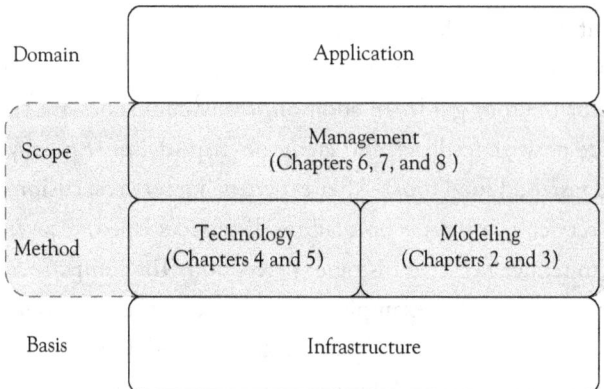

Figure 1.3 Conceptual framework of service mining

fuzzy theory, and so on. Computer science techniques include algorithm, graphical method, petri net, and so forth. IT-oriented researches to solve service problems (e.g., service discovery and recovery) can be classified into this building block.

- **Modeling**

  Modeling includes the areas of statistics and operations research. Statistics includes quantitative methods to analyze services such as regression, SEM, and so on. Modeling also provides a different viewpoint of analytic tools such as the operations management or management science. Modeling the service problems is also a significant and novel issue for service mining, especially in the service domain. Mathematic models also enable companies to look in detail into the service problems.

- **Management**

  Management is at the higher level of service mining framework, which takes into account management issues such as service alliance/cooperation, service branding, service pricing, service innovation, and so on. Traditional discipline of service management mostly investigates the issues of service quality, service failure/recovery, and satisfaction and loyalty of services. In the framework of service mining, the research/practical areas need to go beyond conventional topics. In other words, more management topics such as economics, marketing, and strategy can be included in this level.

- **Application**

  Application specifies the domain of service mining, for example, social network services, IT-enabled services, or traditional services. Other sectors such as telecommunication, restaurant, online service in e-commerce, airline, and so forth, can also make use of application. Service mining aims to solve service problems in a specific domain by combining different technologies or modeling methods.

Table 1.2 synthesizes the elements, research areas of service mining, and relevant researches so far. The trends also reveal leading journals in

Table 1.2 Service mining elements

Element	Service mining areas
Technology[8]	• Artificial intelligence • Computer science
Modeling[9]	• Statistics • Operations management • Management science
Management[10]	• Economics, marketing, strategy • Service alliance/cooperation • Service branding • Service pricing • Service innovation • Service recovery/retention • Service productivity
Application[11]	• Social network services • IT-enabled services • Traditional services

management information systems (MIS) or management fields to investigate service issue for many years. In the level of method, technology and modeling are more technical and mathematical-oriented researches. In the level of scope, more management issues are involved. The focus of service mining is to cover these two levels predominantly. Under the big umbrella of service mining, either technical or managerial researches and practices is applicable.

Looking Back at the Trends

Figure 1.4 demonstrates the trend of service researches between 1990 and 2011 based on the collected data from ISI Web of Knowledge database. There are two key factors to separate service researches in that period are web service and service science. The first period is between 2000 and 2005. The concept of web service was proposed a decade ago. W3C defines a web service as "a software system designed to support interoperable machine-to-machine interaction over a network." Web service research increased dramatically at 2000; in particular, the issue of service discovery was investigated for 5 years. The reason is web services create opportunities for computer science researchers and help explore service researches

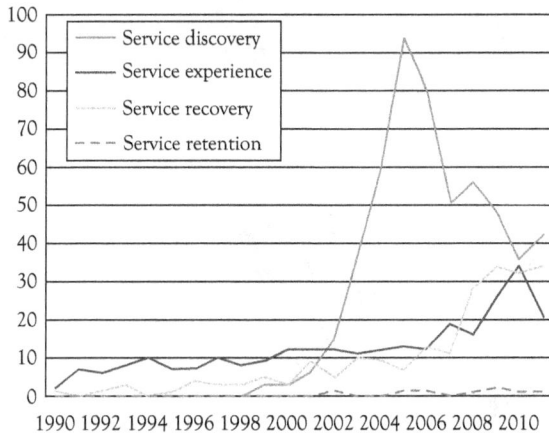

Figure 1.4 Number of service researches

Source: ISI Thomson.

over the Internet. In the first period, the topics of service discovery, experience, and recovery are popular since doing busines over the Internet for companies is well acceptable. However, service research got saturated by 2006. However, service discovery research decreased significantly from 2004 to 2006. Hence, service science provides another opportunity for service researches in the second period (2005 to 2011). The concept of service science, management, and engineering (SSME) was proposed by IBM. The idea is to bring different disciplines together to focus on the service domian.

The topic of web service is mostly investigated by computer science researchers and focuses on Internet service. Since the Internet has become popular and stablized, research of Internet services (web services) decreased. Instead, service science covers not only web services but also traditioanl services by including mutiple disciplines such as engineering, management, and computer science. Service mining aims to provide a new roadmap for service researchers in the coming years (after 2011). The opportunities for service mining research will be broader and deeper. Based on the topics of service discovery, experience, recovery, and retention, researchers can investigate different levels of service research. For example, scholars can apply IT to solve service probems (e.g., technology, model, and management).

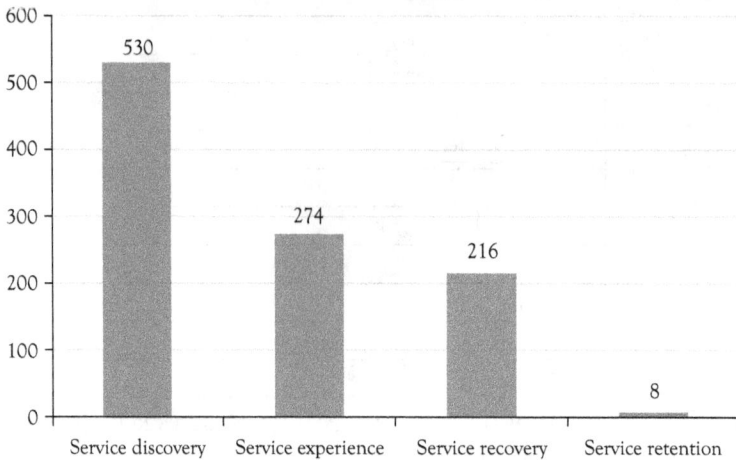

Figure 1.5 Number of service research for four topics

Source: ISI Thomson.

Figure 1.5 illustrates the total number of service researches based on four topics for the past 20 years from the database of ISI web of knowledge. Service discovery is the most researched topic (530) and following by service experience (274), service recovery (216), and service retention/loyalty (8). Since most researchers fully emphasized on how to explore online services and how to make them work (composition) at the beginning of Internet, service discovery is the leading topic that drew attention in the first place. Once the services are explored and mature, service experience and recovery attracts researchers. The numbers in Figure 1.5 reveal that service retention/loyalty (merely 8 researches) still lacks much attention and may be the potential issue for service research in the future.

Looking Forward to the Future

This book proposes a novel research area, service mining, that differs from the notion of service science and provides a comprehensive framework for future researches. Service mining involves five elements: infrastructure, technology, model, management, and application. The iterative process of service mining includes service discovery, service experience, service recovery, and service retention. This book also addresses the research topics among five elements that combine technology and management

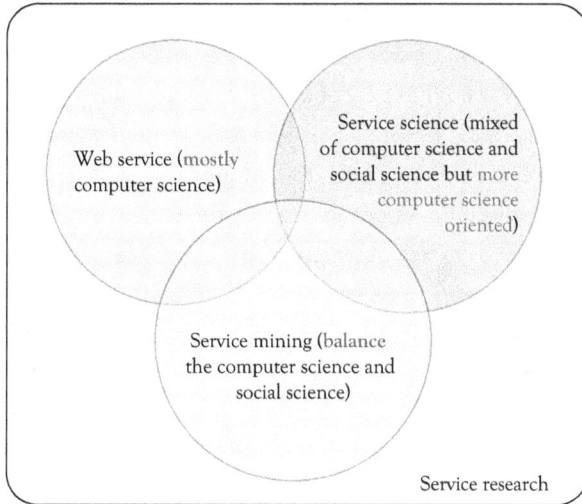

Figure 1.6 Difference between web service, service science, and service mining

perspectives. Compared to web service and service science researches, service mining combines computer science and social science perspectives (Figure 1.6). In early researches on services, most researchers mainly focused on web services owing to the emergence of Internet. Service science combines different perspectives but is still dominated by computer science and engineering areas. Hence, service mining aims to provide a new viewpoint by encompassing computer science and social science equally to contribute to service industry.

According to the statistics of published opportunities, service discovery research is purely computer science oriented while service experience is half computer science and half social science. Meanwhile, pure social science envelopes service recovery and service retention researches. In other words, service mining proves that the combined processes cover two major disciplines and extend to minor subdisciplines such as service, business, and management.

Service mining covers beyond the existing service management and is considered as a branch of service science. Service mining is also different from data mining in the service domain. Based on the entities of service science, this book covers customers (Chapters 2, 5, 6, and 7), service providers (Chapters 3-6), partners (Chapter 4), and employees (Chapters 6 and 8). The concept of data mining focuses on data collected from service sectors. However, the concept of service mining not only investigates data from the service sector but also focuses on the features of services. Mining services is a different goal from mining derived data from services by interacting with human beings. Hence, the process and framework of service mining aims to help researchers from multiple disciplines identify potential opportunities under the umbrella of service research.

This book provides several perspectives on services by utilizing the concept of service mining. Chapter 2 introduces the estimation of customer value of electronic services based on the accounting perspective. Chapter 3 introduces how to price a service based on psychology and marketing perspectives. Chapter 4 introduces the cooperation of electronic services based on value network concept. Chapter 5 introduces the prediction of customer demand on services by using artificial intelligence concepts. Chapter 6 introduces how customers perceive a service brand by optimization. Finally, Chapter 7 introduces the concept of service idealism from customers by prediction.

CHAPTER 2

Mining Customer Value on Services

This chapter introduces the way of predicting customer value on services from the accounting perspective. The method of prediction of customer value is through a modeling approach. This chapter covers the method (modeling), scope (service management), and domain (electronic services) as given in Figure 1.3. In this chapter, service mining is used to help enterprises estimate and predict the customer value on services.

Recently, companies have changed their focus from product-oriented approach within marketing (1960s) to demand-oriented approach within quality improvement (1980s) to an emphasis on customer services, customer loyalty, and customer profitability such that customers drive future strategies and are an important part of the assets of most companies. The benefits of customer loyalty and long-term relationships are no longer a matter of debate.

High customer value will result in superior customer satisfaction and impact customer loyalty.[1] When customers are loyal to products or services, the benefit to the company is enormous. Moreover, enterprises operate more efficiently if they realize maximum value from the consumers and therefore retaining loyal customers is the foundation of profit from either the cost or the revenue perspective; good customer relationships drive the survival of companies.

The significance of customer-centric services is undisputed. A framework for service design was proposed in terms of modeling, designing, and developing e-service systems.[2] The proposed framework also fulfills (semi-)automated value coproduction between the service providers and the customers in a service. In addition, a great deal of research has investigated the effect of customer lifetime value (CLV), but it has focused on the lifetime value of existing customers only, and mostly has focused on physical products or services, rather than on e-services.

In this chapter, we propose a customer value (CV) model, a new model that combines customer and enterprise perspectives to predict customer value for the e-service industry.[3] The CV model complements the existing CLV model by addressing customer value from a different perspective and provides clues to short-term customer value for e-service providers.

A New Customer Value Model for Services

We construct a prediction model for short-term customer value, which is also a type of deterministic model and defines e-services as the coverage of free or charged services over the Internet.[4] In this chapter, we focus on B2C and C2C e-services, such as weather, stock, or auction e-services. The concept of our model is as follows:

$$\text{Customer value} = \frac{\text{Profit}}{\text{Time usage}} \qquad (2.1)$$

The concept is separated into two blocks: profit and time usage. Profit uses the variables of original profit and the ones that influence profit. The variable of original profit is the same concept as that of CLV, which estimates the value that customers can create for firms over the customers' lifetimes. The additional variable of influence on profit takes into account both the customer and the enterprise perspectives. In the enterprise perspective, we use reach rate as the primary indicator for advertisements over the Internet and portals (e.g., Yahoo), which may include free or paid e-services, because the reach rate is easy to collect for portals. In considering the customer perspective, we take into account the effect of perceived quality for e-services—that is, the difference between expectation and perception—and consider time usage to be appropriate to access cost because of the characteristics of e-services. Hence, our model estimates the customer value per unit of time and is different from previous models that predict CLV per unit of cost.

We define the variables in our model as shown in Eq. (2.1) and Table 2.1. Time usage indicates the time required for a customer to use

Table 2.1 Definition of profit and time usage

Component	Definition	Measurement
Time usage	The time for a customer to use e-services	The time required from the beginning to the end of using e-services
Profit	The profit created by customers for the enterprise	1. Enterprise: Reach rate 2. Customer: The perceived e-service quality. Additional profits are generated when PS > ES and original profits may be reduced when PS < ES

e-services, measured from the beginning to the end of a transaction. Profit denotes the net value of revenue that is generated by customers using e-services, measured by (1) reach rate of advertising (from the enterprise) and (2) perceived e-service quality (from the customer). Reach rate may result in extra benefits for the enterprise, and any gap between perceived quality and expected quality will impact the additional benefits; if the gap is negative, the additional benefits will decline and if the gap is positive, the additional benefits will increase. Hence, our model proposes that customer value is a function of reach rate and perceived quality per unit of time required to use the e-service. This concept differs from conventional measures of CLV, which take into account only the financial perspective.

Eq. (2.1) can be unfolded into Eq. (2.2), which extends time usage and profit to the customer and the enterprise perspective, respectively (Table 2.2), such that

$$CV = \frac{NV\left[1 + \sum W_i R_m + \sum (PS - ES)\right]}{TU} \qquad (2.2)$$

where CV denotes the profit generated by a customer per unit of time, NV is the net value of revenue, R is the ratio of information that is delivered to the customers (also known as reach rate), m indicates different types of media (e.g., Yahoo, MSN), W is the weight for each media, PS is the perceived value of e-service(s) for a customer, ES is the expected value of e-service(s) for a customer, and TU is the average time required for a customer to use e-service(s).

Table 2.2 *Definition of all variables in the model*

Variable	Customer value	Net value of revenue	Reach rate	Medium	Weight	Perception of service	Expectation of service	Time usage
Symbol	CV	NV	R	M	W	PS	ES	TU
Definition	The profit generated by a customer per unit of time	The net income; the income minus cost	The rate of information delivered to customers	Different types of media	The weight for each medium	The perceived value of e-service(s) for a customer	The expected value of e-service(s) for a customer	Average time usage for a customer

Customer Segmentation

We segment customers based on profit (enterprise perspective) and satisfaction (customer perspective). Profit indicates the total revenue that customers generated in the past, which is also the concept of NV in our model. Satisfaction denotes the difference between perception and expectation, which is the difference between ES and PS in our model. We segment four types of customers, based on high and low profit and positive and negative satisfaction (Figure 2.1): Defecting customers, consuming customers, potential customers, and best customers.

Best customers generate high profits and have positive satisfaction since positive satisfaction results in high loyalty and repeat purchases. For customers in this category, companies need to provide personal services in order to maintain customer loyalty and retain these valuable customers. Potential customers generate low profits but have positive satisfaction. Customers in this category are satisfied that the e-services they use meet their needs, and they have a good image of the company. Although the profit from these customers is low, companies have a significant opportunity to increase profits from these customers, so the companies need to maintain positive satisfaction in order to increase the customers' loyalty and create more profits. Consuming customers generate high profits but have negative satisfaction. Customers in this category are at risk for attrition, so companies need to increase use time for these customers in

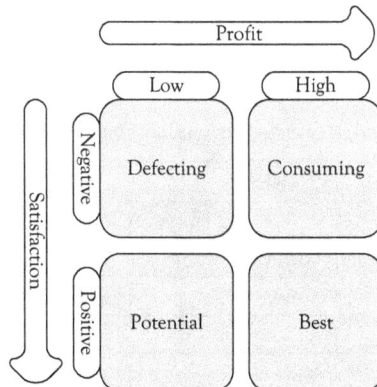

Figure 2.1 The matrix for customer segmentation

order to raise the satisfaction and loyalty and transfer the customers from the consuming type to the best type. Defecting customers generate low profits and have negative satisfaction. In this category, customers used the e-services for a short time and created limited profits. These are the most difficult customers—and perhaps the most costly to retain. If a company decides to invest in them, it should investigate the reasons for their dissatisfaction, correct any shortcomings, and communicate those shortcomings to the customers in the hope that they will eventually become more satisfied and more profitable.

An Example of Simulation

The real data is not easy and mostly needs a long time period to collect. This book simulated customer behavior based on real-world patterns. The simulated data is closer to what we are looking for and explainable in the model. We created four scenarios in terms of NV, TU, and ES–PS. Each of the four types of customer (best, potential, consuming, and defecting) is used to simulate four scenarios (Table 2.3). The simulated historical data (from past to present) for NV and TU trends gradually up in scenario I. The simulated historical data for NV trends gradually up, and TU trends gradually down in scenario II. The simulated historical data for NV trends gradually down and TU trends gradually up in scenario III. The simulated historical data for NV and TU both trend gradually down in scenario IV. We also simulated positive differences for best/potential customers and negative differences for consuming/defecting customers. Figure 2.2 illustrates the trend of historical data and predicted

Table 2.3 Simulated scenarios for each type of customer

	NV	ES–PS	TU	NV	ES–PS	TU
Scenario	Best/potential customers			Consuming/defecting customers		
I	Up	Positive	Up	Up	Negative	Up
II	Up	Positive	Down	Up	Negative	Down
III	Down	Positive	Up	Down	Negative	Up
IV	Down	Positive	Down	Down	Negative	Down

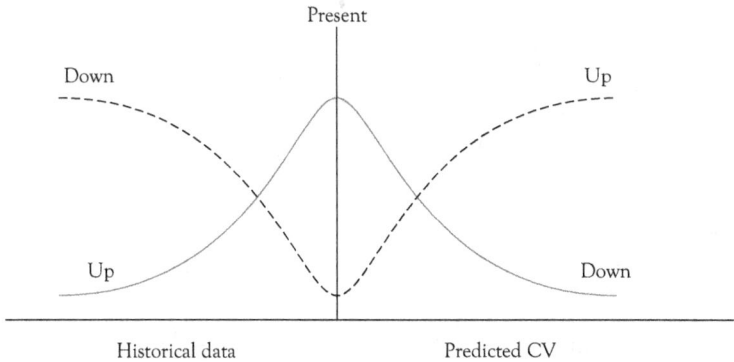

Figure 2.2 The relationship between historical data and predicted CV

customer value, which is reversed in the predicting process. That is, if the trend for historical data is down (up), the trend for predicted CV will be up (down).

The simulated results (Figure 2.3) reveal that the best result is scenario II and the worst result is scenario III, while scenarios I and IV give similar results. The estimated percentage of the distribution of customer value for each type is 48% for scenario II, 21% for scenarios I and IV, and 10% for scenario III. Thus, scenario II is superior to scenario I and scenario IV is superior to scenario III. The results also show that best type, not surprisingly, has the best customer value, the defecting type has the worst, and the consuming and potential types are in between, with the consuming type superior to the potential type in our simulation. In short, our simulation generates 16 different results with four types of customers and four types of scenarios. The best result is the best type of customer (high profit, high satisfaction) in scenario II (historical data for NV trends gradually up, and TU trends gradually down) and the worst result is the defecting type of customer (low profit, low satisfaction) in scenario III (historical data for NV trends gradually down and TU trends gradually up). The best result of the defecting type, in scenario II, is superior to that of the potential type in scenarios I and III and the consuming type in scenario III. Thus, defecting customers still need to be taken into account in terms of their potential for creating more profit.

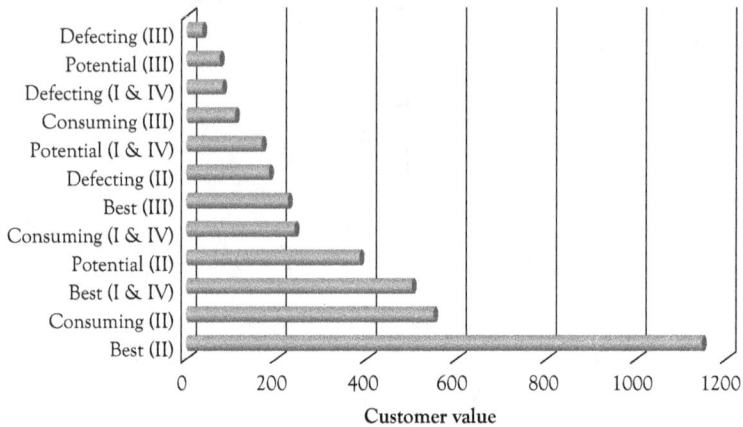

Figure 2.3 All results of the simulation

Insights From New Model of Customer Value

The model by which to measure customer value has changed with the onset of technology revolution. In this section, we compare the difference between our CV model and the existing CLV model (Table 2.4). The extant literature has investigated the relationships among products, service quality, and customer value in direct marketing, but we propose a different perspective of a model for customer value in the Internet environment.[5] The proposed model combines two perspectives to predict future customer value based on historical data. The model which provides clues for measuring customer value is simpler and easier to understand than existing mathematical models and takes into account e-service quality, which is often difficult to measure and quantify. Some of the extant research has emphasized the relationship between the customer and service quality, but it has not predicted customer value.[6]

Existing researches estimated CLV from financial indicators and strengthened CLV by proposing a variety of marketing strategies.[9] In predicting customer value over the short-term (within 12 months), our CV model is the complement of CLV, which predicts long-term customer value (a few years). Our results also support the idea that e-services have the potential to impact customer value.

Generally, reach rate is the most useful measure with which companies can execute marketing strategies. Some research has indicated that

Table 2.4 Major differences between CV and CLV

	Customer value (CV)	Customer lifetime value (CLV)
Environment	Internet (e-services)	Physical (Products/Services)
Concept	Utilize e-service quality and reach rate to measure customer value	Evaluate CLV
Perspective	Customer and enterprise	Enterprise
Difference	Short-term prediction	Long-term prediction
Advantages[7]	1. Financial perspective (net value of revenue) 2. Designed for e-services 3. Combination of customer and enterprise perspectives 4. Easy to apply	1. Financial perspective (Dwyer, 1989) 2. Utilizes customer retention rate (Nadeem, 2006) 3. Customer value table (Mulhern, 1999) 4. Need more information to apply
Limitations[8]	1. A limited model 2. E-service quality is not easy to measure 3. Ignores the differences among various types of markets	1. Complicated computation 2. Ignores satisfaction (Nadeem, 2006) 3. Appropriate only for a physical environment

word-of-mouth can affect CLV, but problems in the measures may be caused by over-involvement of customers (e.g., ethical crises). The current work considers how advertising influences customer satisfaction/loyalty and places reach rate as a variable in the model. We focus on e-services that customers can consume over the Internet, but the proposed model can be applied to other industries as well; future research can investigate different types of markets (e.g., the completely perfect market) in order to observe and predict changes in CV.

The CV model and the CLV model both come from the customer perspective, but CLV measures CLV without prediction while the CV model provides an avenue by which to consider customer and enterprise perspective simultaneously. Thus, the CV model not only complements the CLV but also assists enterprises in identifying customer value and generating superior benefits.

In this chapter, the concept of service mining provides a different perspective to look at customer value on services. Traditionally, CLV is used in accounting to predict customer value for better management. The proposed customer value model is a new viewpoint to refine customer value especially on services. By modeling customer value, enterprises can get closer and better understanding of customers on services. This also results in superior service management and dealing with customer responses.

CHAPTER 3

Mining the Price of Service

This chapter introduces how to estimate the price of service based on customer-perceived value. The method to price the services is through a modeling approach using behavioral psychology as the basis. This chapter covers the method (modeling), scope (service pricing), and domain (electronic services) in Figure 1.3. In this chapter, service mining is used to help enterprises get a better understanding of fair price of services.

The development of information technology has triggered the transformation of traditional services concept into the new array of online services (electronic service). E-services reduce costs and enhance the efficiency to build strong customer relationships.[1] E-service is defined as "providing services through an electronic network."[2] Research on traditional services mostly focus on quality issues, particularly E-SERVQUAL was proposed to measure service quality, and some devised constructs were used to measure online shopping quality.[3] However, the synthesized perspective of pricing and quality issues is still scant. In addition, existing literature on pricing issues also focuses on digital products. The essentiality of e-services is to provide a customer-centric quality of services, which is simultaneously influenced by a customer's perceived quality.[4] Hence this research considers e-service quality to build an e-service pricing model.

In service marketing, the difficulty of pricing services is higher than that of products. A comprehensive e-service pricing method is also scant. The traditional cost-oriented pricing approach is not applicable to the e-service domain due to the features of e-services (e.g., storable and dividable).[5] Furthermore, studies have frequently investigated the relationships between price, quality, and perceived value to examine consumer intentions based on existing research.[6] In this chapter, we seek to propose a pricing model for a particular e-service based on customer perceived quality and observe the relationship between price and the perceived value.

In other words, the proposed pricing model generates an appropriate price and examines the influence of the perceived value from the price.

According to a report by InsightXplorer in Taiwan (August 2009), the market share of blogs in Taiwan is as follows: Wretch (57.9%), Yahoo (14.7%), Pixnet (5.6%), Windows Live Spaces (4.4%), and Yam (3.8%). We collected data from existing paid e-services. Yahoo and Yam provide free online space to registered users, and Windows Live Spaces provides free limited space to registered users. Wretch and Pixnet both provide free and paid memberships. Meanwhile, Wretch has the most members in Taiwan (officially 6.5 million users) compared to Pixnet (officially 1.45 million users), including 5% paid members. Hence, we selected Wretch (http://www.wretch.cc/) as an example to test the proposed model.

Discovering Service Price

In this chapter, we investigate two parts: the pricing model and the perceived value, and propose an e-service pricing model based on perceived e-service quality, as well as utilizing transaction utility theory as the basis to discuss the relationship between price and the perceived value for e-services. We use the concept of the extended cost-oriented pricing approach for traditional services to build a new pricing model, which is based on e-service quality. In Eq. (3.1), C is the total cost of an e-service (i.e., fixed cost and variable cost), GP is the expected profit of the e-service, and Q is the score of the customer-perceived e-service quality based on e-SERVQUAL. P^{a} is the revised price, and P^{m} is the average market price.

$$P^{\alpha} = P^{m} + (C + \mathrm{GP}) * (1 + Q) \tag{3.1}$$

Eq. (3.1) can be divided into two parts: pricing basis (C and GP) and user benefit (Q). The idea is to consider the average market price (P) and perceived e-service quality simultaneously to generate a new price. In the pricing basis part, this study defines cost to include variable cost and fixed cost as a monetary value. A variable cost indicates the changeable cost of a specific e-service based the increment or decrement of users, such as maintenance cost. Fixed cost indicates the total amount of fixed costs of a specific e-service in a time period. Expected profit is the financial benefit that an e-service provider aims to gain in a time period.

In the user benefit part, this book utilizes seven constructs from e-SERVQUAL (efficiency, fulfillment, reliability, privacy, responsiveness, compensation, and contact) to measure customer-perceived e-service quality, and to estimate the gap between perception and expectation. We define the concept as shown in Eq. (3.2). i stands for i th construct, P_i indicates the perceived e-service quality of the i-th construct, and E_i is the expected e-service quality of the i th construct.

$$q_i = \left(P_i - E_i \right) \tag{3.2}$$

We employ multiattribute utility theory (MAUT) to sum the score of each construct as a final score. The customer also provides the weight of each construct simultaneously. MAUT is a decision-based approach for evaluating the value of a product. Each user has his or her own value and weight based on perception. Eq. (3.3) shows the concept of MAUT for this research. In this study, n is equal to 7, which indicates the seven constructs. w_i indicates the relative value of weight for the i-th construct compared to other constructs from customer perception and $\sum_{i=1}^{n} w_i = 1$.

$$Q = \sum_{i=1}^{n} \left(w_i * q_i \right) \tag{3.3}$$

In addition to the price, we investigate the relationship between price and perceived value, employing transaction utility theory to estimate the perceived value of a specific e-service based on the generated price. Transaction utility theory employs two functions as the basis: value function and utility function. The concept of transaction utility theory is shown in Eq. (3.4), in which $v(\bar{p} - p)$ indicates the acquisition utility, which is the gap between actual paid price ($\bar{p}$) and perceived value equal to product z ($\bar{p}$) for purchasing product z. $v(-p: -p^*)$ represents transaction utility,

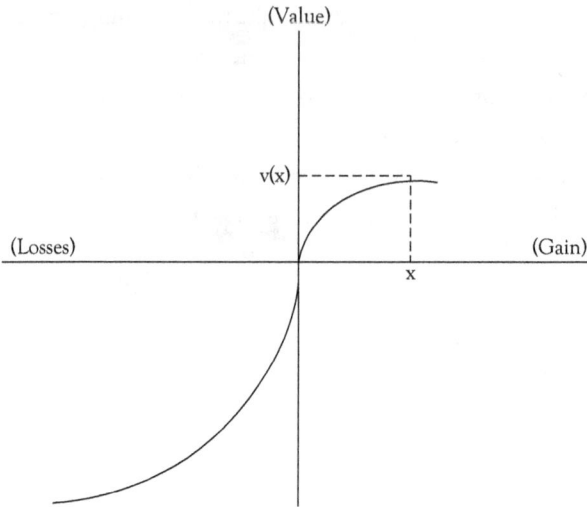

Figure 3.1 Value function

Source: Thaler (1985).

which is difference between actual paid price (p) and reference price (p^*) for Product z. Hence, the total utility is $W(z, p, p^*)$.

$$W(z, p, p^*) = v(\overline{p}, -p) + v(-p : -p^*) \tag{3.4}$$

The original definition for transaction utility theory is the utility of a specific product. We consider e-service to be a type of information product that can be applied to this model. Thus, Product z can be changed to e-service z. p is the actual paid price for purchasing e-service z, p^* is the reference price for z, which is also the average paid price for z or similar e-services, and $\overline{p}$ is the perceived value for purchasing the e-service z. Additionally, the value function is also applied to the proposed model, as shown in Figure 3.1. The value function presents the mapping relationship between value and gains/losses. This study investigates and analyzes the changes of perceived value from the generated price.

An Example to Price Services

We utilized a simple questionnaire to collect data from paid members (silver, golden, and super golden). The purpose was to obtain the expectation and perception of e-service quality between prepurchase and postpurchase of the members. We utilized a 7-point Likert scale, with a score of 1 indicating "very poor" to 7 indicating "very good." The expected price and equivalent value were obtained simultaneously as a monetary value. The question to obtain the expected price was, "What was the expected price for this e-service before purchasing the membership?" The question to obtain the equivalent value was, "What is the price based on perceived e-service performance after purchasing the membership?"

A total of 105 samples were collected via an online sampling approach. The valid number of samples was 100, and the valid response rate was 95%. The ratio of gender was even for males and females. The age of members varied between 20 and 25 (70%), and 26 and 30 (21%). Member education levels ranged from university/college (58%) to graduate students (34%). Paying members were mostly students (48%). The income of members was chiefly below 10,000 TWD (36%).

Mining New Prices of Services

We separated 100 data points into six categories with respect to the valid period and membership price as follows: (1) 21% for 30 days silver ($2.75), (2) 42% for 365 days silver ($15.6), (3) 7% for 30 days golden ($5.88), (4) 24% for 365 days golden ($31.25), (5) 2% for 365 days super silver ($64.5), and (6) 4% for super golden ($125). However, the number of samples for super silver and super golden members was insufficient. Therefore, the analysis was mainly based on silver and golden members. The usage of e-services for 30 days and 365 days for silver or golden members is the same. Therefore, the discussion is combined based on the different periods of membership instead of the types of membership:

1. **Silver 30 days**

   The actual price for this type of membership is $2.75. The average expected price from respondents is $1.8. The average equivalent value is $2.53. The new estimated price is $1.94.

2. **Silver 365 days**

   The actual price for this type of membership is $15.6. The average expected price from respondents is $10.5. The average equivalent value is $10.94. The new estimated price is $4.69.

3. **Golden 30 days**

The actual price for this type of membership is $5.88. The average expected price from respondents is $5.13. The average equivalent value is $5.59. The new estimated price is $5.31.

4. **Golden 365 days**

The actual price for this type of membership is $31.25. The average expected price from respondents is $21.53. The average equivalent value is $19.97. The new estimated price is $9.38.

The results revealed that the average perceived e-service quality of silver and golden members are both negative. The negative effect of perceived quality may generate a low estimated price. Figure 3.2 shows the comparison of the negative effects of average perceived quality. The average number of differences between expectation and perception for e-service quality are −1.3 (30 days silver), −1.7 (365 days silver), −1.1 (30 days golden), and −1.7 (365 days golden). The negative effect of 30 days silver is −30%, which is derived from the sum of 1 and −1.3. Therefore, the total effect of the perceived e-service quality on new price estimation is merely 70%. The impact for 365 days silver and 365 days golden is significant, which results in −70% perceived e-service quality. The perceived e-service quality is extremely low (both −1.7). The minus effect of 30 days golden is low, which only reduces 10% for the new price estimation.

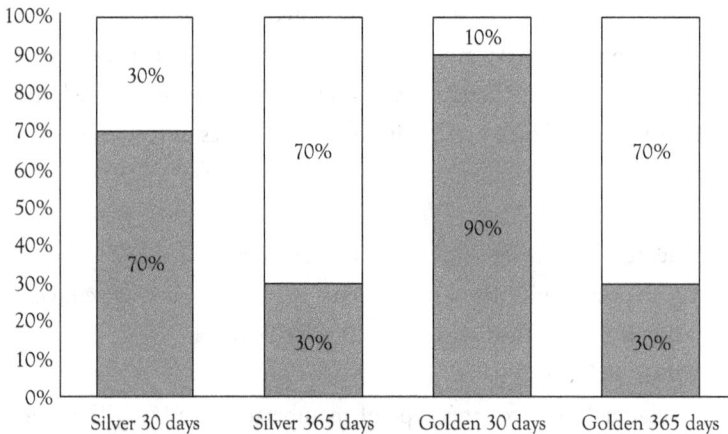

Figure 3.2 Comparison of the negative effects of average perceived e-service quality

Members who paid for 365 days (silver or golden) may expect a higher e-service quality compared to members who paid for 30 days. However, the results reveal that the perceived e-service quality is significantly lower than expected.

Insights From Re-Modeling Service Prices

Existing studies mostly investigated the definition, scope, and quality of e-services. The pricing model for e-services still remains scant in the related literature. Although pricing models for traditional services are addressed, the appropriateness for applying them in e-services still requires verification. We proposed a quality-based e-service pricing model, utilizing e-SERVQUAL as the basis to measure e-service quality and combine MAUT to estimate the price. The results reveal that new price can increase perceived value from negative to positive. The new price is also closer to the reference point of the consumers. Furthermore, we investigated the causal relations between perceived quality, price, and perceived value, instead of price, perceived quality, and perceived value, as is the traditional perspective. This book also verified the relationship between old price and new price. The results confirm that price may be the intermediary between perceived quality and perceived value.

In this chapter, the concept of service mining provides a different viewpoint to recheck the service price. In the traditional marketing perspective, pricing methods are taken into account the expected profit. However, services are different from products as especially customer perceptions are different. Hence, dynamic pricing concept is used to explore the appropriate service price for various customers. By remodeling the service price, enterprises may have a different mindset to implement differential pricing. The profits will also improve increasingly in the end.

CHAPTER 4

Mining Cooperation of Services

This chapter introduces how to use information technology to discover appropriate electronic service partners. Fuzzy theory, which is widely used in artificial intelligence, is used to investigate the fitness between two service providers. This chapter covers the method (technology), scope (service cooperation), and domain (electronic services) given in Figure 1.3. In this chapter, service mining is used to assist enterprises recheck the appropriateness of service partners scientifically.

Due to economic development, the structures of industries have changed. The service industry has recently become the economic core of every country (Figure 4.1). The number is more than 70% in Europe and the United States. The concept of e-service recently extended the business model of e-commerce.[1] E-service not only reduces cost, but also increases the efficiency of companies.[2]

E-service can be divided into two dimensions: category process (B2B, B2C, and C2C) and delivery process (physical, digital, and pure services).[3] Based on our knowledge, most users access Internet portals frequently throughout the day (e.g., Yahoo). An Internet portal is the gate that connects websites around the world, providing all types of services, such as weather, finance, dictionary, or navigation. However, these services are furnished by other allied companies. The existing literature mostly investigates traditional companies.[4] Nevertheless, research regarding cooperations in the e-service industry is still scant.

The purpose of strategic alliance is to reduce costs and risks, acquire resources and knowledge, or enter foreign countries. A strategic alliance may fail. According to a report from McKinsey, 60% of all strategic alliances have failed. The evaluation of a strategic alliance is extremely significant. Existing literature merely focuses on the demand of enterprises

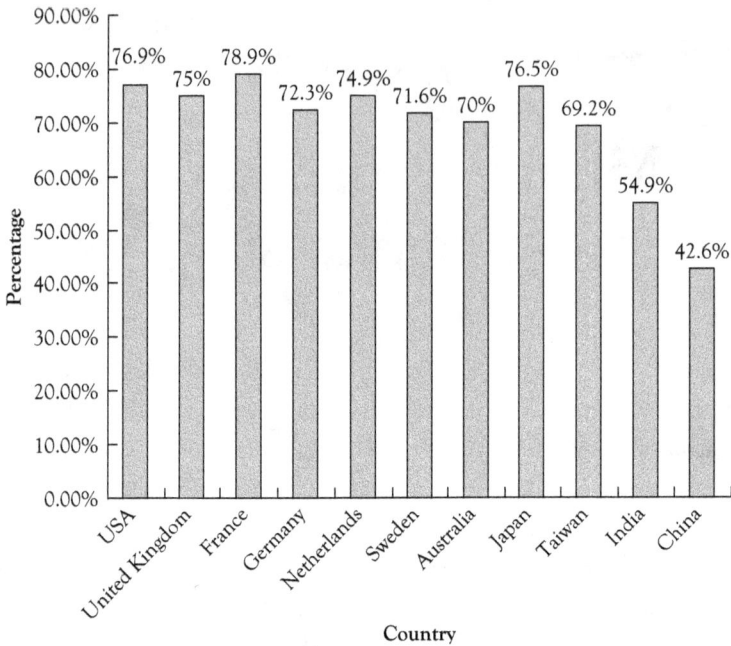

Figure 4.1 Ratio of service to GDP

Source: The World Factbook (2009).

to earn profits. In this chapter, we investigate the alliance of e-service from the customer's perspective, utilizing the concept by Allee (2000) to construct a value network of cooperation, including product, service, and intangible asset.[5] In addition, complement skills, cultures, and goal compatibility are considered to be crucial for alliances.[6] Financial assets, technology, degree of willingness to share, and capital asset were also the criteria for choosing partners.[7] The goal of an alliance is to obtain mutual benefits.[8] The appropriateness of an alliance is also significant for two allied companies. The performance of an alliance is an indicator to measure the appropriateness of two allied companies.

In this chapter, we aim to trigger an alliance from the customer's perspective. In other words, we emphasize the cooperation between e-service providers. In the environment of e-commerce, a customer's needs are significant to firms that can help them obtain profit. According to the subjective theory of value, the value of a product and service is generated by customer needs. Thus, this study recognizes customer needs by delivering value in an e-service alliance. Cooperation features also vary depending on the customers. We consider customer assessment for all features (e.g., score and weight), and use them as the basis for e-service cooperation. To solve this ambiguous problem, we use fuzzy theory to collect the customer perception of value in an accurate manner.

A Value Network Based Cooperation

We use a value network to present the delivered value between an e-service provider and customer. A value network is an analytic viewpoint for enterprises.[9] The node in the network represents a company or a customer. The line to connect two nodes represents the delivered value. The network that enfolds all nodes and lines is the value network. Meanwhile, the tangible and intangible values are also considered in the value network. A tangible value indicates product, service, and profit. An intangible value, includes knowledge regarding process, technology, and collaborative design. The value of a value network comprises product, service, profit, knowledge, or intangible benefit.

Figure 4.2 shows that A is the website and B is the possible company for cooperation. This study examined a portal (i.e., Yahoo) as the major company that may cooperate with other e-service providers (e.g., weather and finance). A portal is an access point for the Internet and provides fast and updated information.[10] Thus, the value of a portal is convenience. Consumers can generate traffic for a website and attract advertising income. Furthermore, Company B provides e-services to consumers and earns an income.[11] For example, if B is an online bookstore, the delivered value is book and knowledge. We examine the value from an e-service cooperation viewpoint and evaluate the perception of consumers on satisfaction.

Case Illustration: Yahoo! Online Dictionary

Figure 4.3 demonstrates the value network of Yahoo! online dictionary in Taiwan. Online dictionaries can overcome the problem of finding appropriate meanings of translated sentences when learning a second language.[12] Hence, the correctness of an online dictionary is very important for online users because it provides a picture of a reliable service. There is the option

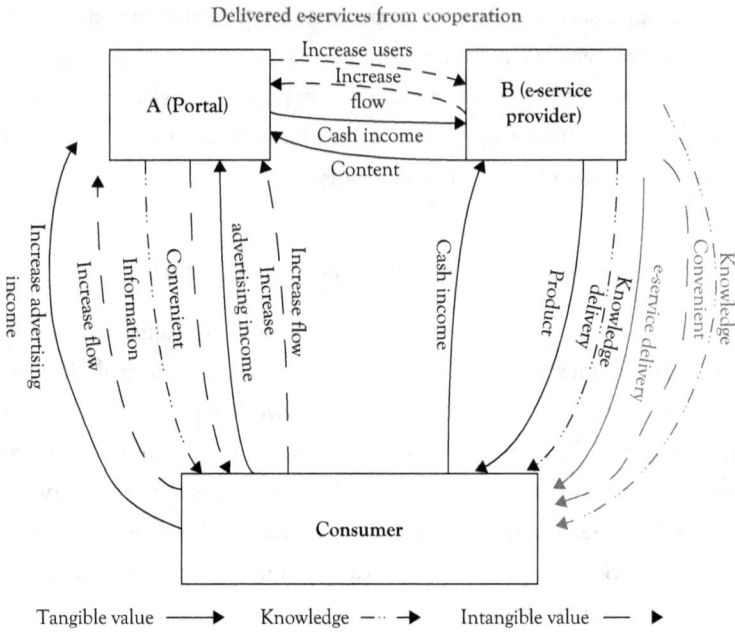

Figure 4.2 Value network

Source: Allee (2000).

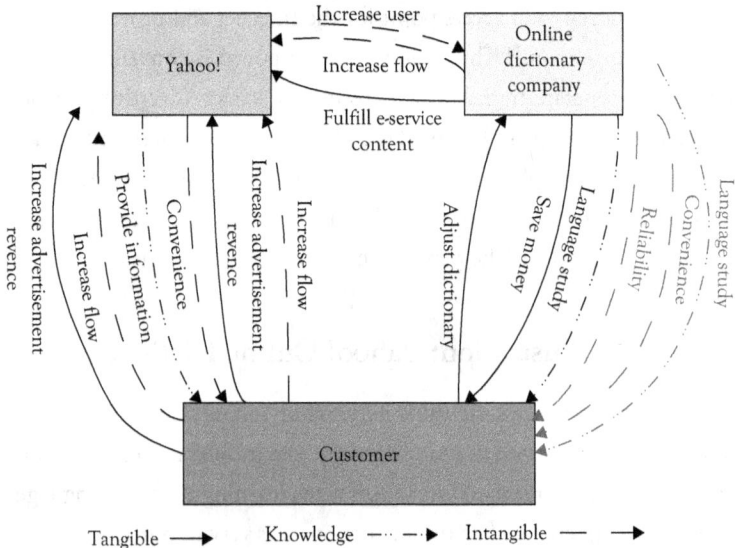

Figure 4.3 Value network of Yahoo! online dictionary

of learning multiple languages via the Internet.[13] Specifically, a large number of online dictionaries furnish the pronunciation of each word over the Internet. This research synthesized three significant criteria for online dictionaries as the major value (reliability, convenience, and language study), and extended them to seven subcriteria based on the literature.

We collected 100 samples, and only invited people who had the experience using online dictionaries (Figure 4.4). The results show that the reliability of fuzzy satisfaction for Yahoo!/Google's online dictionary is 0.5274, 0.7254, 0.9008, which is higher than Yahoo!/Dr. Eye (0.4113, 0.6041, 0.7906). The two subcriteria of Yahoo!/Google's online dictionary are all higher than those of Yahoo!/Dr. Eye. This research discovered that the functions (explanation and translation) and correctness are similar for Dr. Eye and Google's online dictionary. The only difference is that Google permits users to search for other meanings or explanations over the Internet. The extended search function is convincing for users and makes up for the shortage of the scope of the dictionary. However, Yahoo! enables users to extend their search on the basis of knowledge, instead of websites. The correctness of sources is however questionable. Therefore, users might consider Google's online dictionary to be superior to that of Dr. Eye.

The results show that the convenience of fuzzy satisfaction for Yahoo!/Google's online dictionary is 0.6029, 0.8028, 0.933, which is higher than that of Yahoo!/Dr. Eye (0.5177, 0.7142, 0.8838). The two subcriteria of Yahoo!/Google's online dictionary are all higher than those of Yahoo!/Dr. Eye. The accessibility is similar due to the convenience of the Internet. However, the usability is different. Dr. Eye separates its dictionary and translation into two webpages, and Google's online dictionary integrates two functions into a webpage. In addition, Yahoo! also embedded unrelated advertisements in the online dictionary webpage, which may render it messy. Therefore, users possibly prefer an easy and clean interface when using online dictionaries.

The results show that the fuzzy satisfaction for Yahoo!/Google's online dictionary is 0.5577, 0.7570, 0.9172, which is higher than that of Yahoo!/Dr. Eye (0.4199, 0.6136, 0.8055). The three subcriteria of Yahoo!/Google's online dictionary are all higher than those of Yahoo!/Dr. Eye. The integrity of content revealed that Google's online dictionary is superior

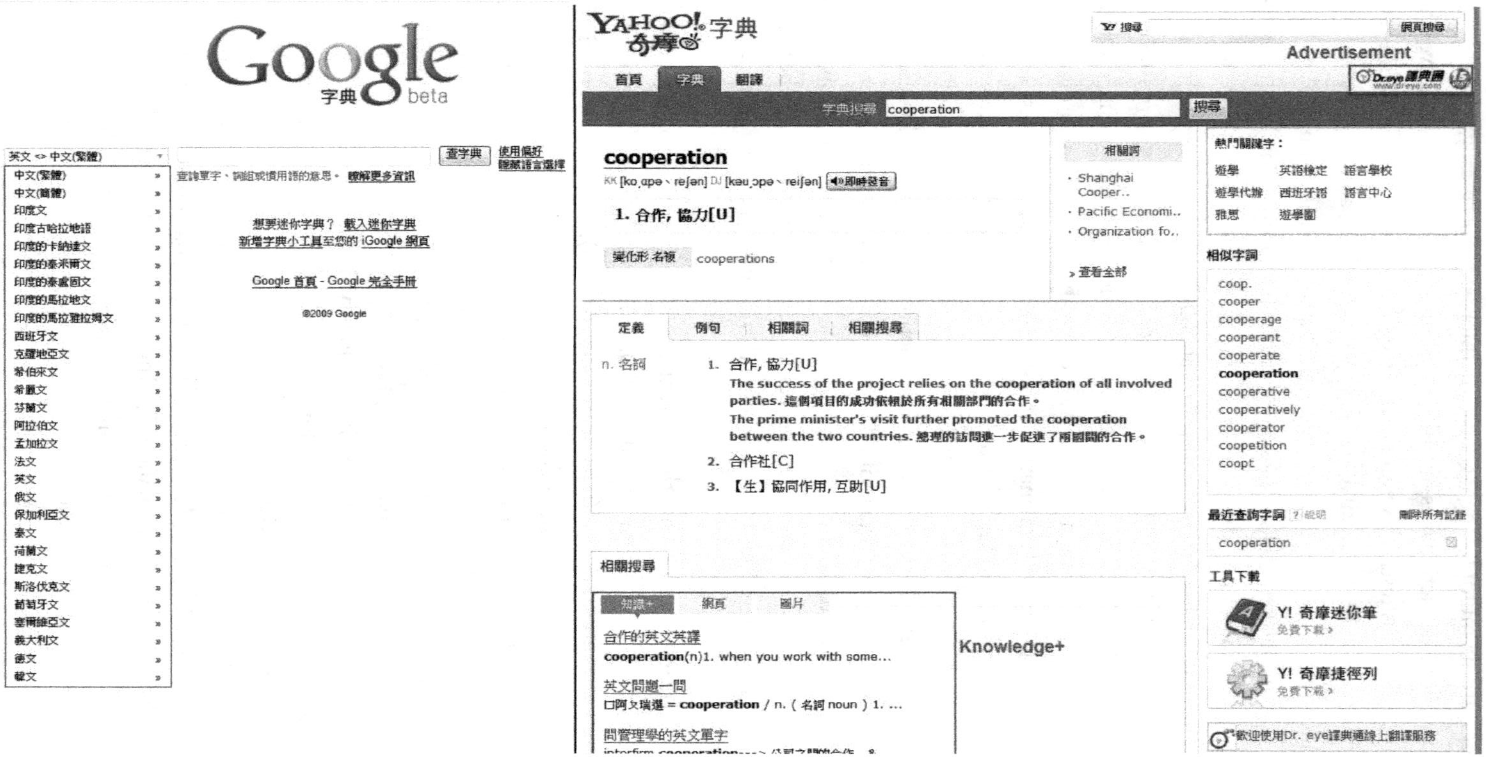

Figure 4.4 *Google's online dictionary and Yahoo!/Dr. Eye online dictionary in Taiwan*

to that of Dr. Eye because Google allows extended search via the Internet. The correctness of pronunciation in English is similar. Specifically, Google enables the user access multiple languages (58 countries) for its dictionary and translation. Therefore, this study inferred that users prefer Google's online dictionary compared to that of Dr. Eye.

According to the research, the fuzzy satisfaction of each criterion can be transformed into a triangular membership function.[14] Hence, reliability = {0.6031/A, 0.7216/B}, convenience = {0.7097/A, 0.7912/B}, and language study = {0.6133/A, 0.7505/B}. The results are subsequently multiplied by weight. The results are as follows:

- Reliability × 0.551648 = {0.3327/A, 0.3981/B}
- Convenience × 0.307928 = {0.2185/A, 0.2436/B}
- Language study × 0.140424 = {0.0861/A, 0.1054/B}

We used a minimum number to determine the decision (D) = {0.0861/A, 0.1054/B}. Hence, the best decision is B (0.1054), which means that users consider Google's online dictionary to be the optimal partner for Yahoo!. According to a report from AC Nielsen on January 2011, the number of persons-times for Google is 361542000, and Yahoo! is 234449000. Users utilize dictionaries in their default homepage. Since the number of persons-times for Google is higher than that of Yahoo!, this research inferred high usage results in high reputation and positive evaluation for Google.

The results of this case study reveal that the optimal partner for Yahoo! is Google's online dictionary. However, the current partner is Dr. Eye, and not Google. Yahoo! and Google are competitors, though Yahoo! is a portal and Google is a search engine. According to the co-opetition, a chance still exists for cooperation when still in competition. The goal is to create more value and benefit with sacrifices and contributions. In this case, Yahoo! benefits from Google (establishing a quality online dictionary), though Google does not benefit from Yahoo!. In addition, a joint goal with trust is necessary for both companies under a competition/cooperation framework. In this case, the goals of two firms are completely different. Yahoo! earns profits while Google provides quality and free online services. Hence, the cooperation between the companies is impossible in their current state. The results provide insight for Yahoo! that the quality of its existing online dictionary is significant to users. In summation, Yahoo! must improve the quality and user interface (remove advertisements) of Dr. Eye from its portal.

Implications for Mining Cooperative Services

Companies must recognize what type of value they can convey to customers or what customers want when they are offered a service. This research used the concept of a value network to reveal the value between customers and e-service providers. For example, reliability, convenience, and language study are major values for Yahoo!. Firms can conduct surveys and review literature to discover key values. The significance of a value can also guide companies to allocate resources efficiently. Once a value is identified, the furnished e-service can appropriately be delivered to customers. Thus, this study proves the significance of a value network and can help enterprises recognize their value.

Selecting potential partners or evaluating existing partners are significant processes for companies. Strategic planning after cooperation is also essential. Specifically, the assessment of current partners is necessary to discover problems. For Yahoo!, the results reveal that Google's online dictionary is superior to that of Dr. Eye, which is its existing partner. The results also help managers consider changing partners or reexamining the value for improvement. Based on the concept of competition, firms can also consider cooperation under competition. Hence, this research provides a different perspective from the customer viewpoint for e-service cooperation.

Existing literature on strategic alliance chiefly focused on traditional industries. The selection and evaluation of partners also relies on financial assessment. The goal is to increase profit through cooperation. This research devised and applied fuzzy theory to provide a customer-oriented concept for cooperation in an e-service environment. Existing e-services are mostly free. Thus, companies can consider more customers responses to appeal to more potential customers. That is, companies should consider customers when selecting partners for cooperation, which differs from the traditional approach.

In this chapter, the concept of service mining provides a different viewpoint to recheck the appropriateness between service providers. Alliance and cooperation are necessary to obtain higher benefit and profit. Discovering appropriate partners is extremely important in service industry because service is dynamic and the synergy of service cooperation is difficult to measure. Hence, using scientific method to quantifying the appropriateness between service providers is useful. By reexamining the cooperation from customer viewpoint, companies can understand which partner is worth to cooperate and earn more profit. The synergy may also be amplified by selecting right partners on services.

CHAPTER 5

Mining Services in Customer Relationship Management

This chapter proposes how to use modeling behavior to predict services based on customer demands. The methods that are employed to forecast potential services are Bayesian theorem and Markov chain. This chapter covers the method (modeling), scope (customer service usage), and domain (electronic services) as given in Figure 1.3. In this chapter, service mining is used to assist enterprises better understand what the customer demands and what the appropriate services are.

Due to recent developments in the increasing use of Internet, consumer behavior has changed and new needs have emerged. Enterprises devoted to combining new technologies with traditional service concepts have created a new type of service called e-service. Firms attempting to deliver products or services electronically do so to enhance operational efficiency and profit. Customer relationship management (CRM) shows particular potential as a bourgeoning e-service. In a traditional business model, profits can be enhanced by 25% to 80% by increasing customer loyalty by just 5%. A 1% increase in the customer retention rate has a 5% influence on the company's profit.[1] The cost required to discover a new customer is six to seven times greater than that required to retaining existing customers.[2] E-services offer an additional opportunity to retain customers and improve customer loyalty in a highly effective and efficient manner.

According to a report from Bain & Company (www.bain.com), the average annual rate of customer loss is approximately 20% to 30% for U.S. enterprises. Even among top 500 enterprises, at least half of the customer base is lost every 5 years. Most existing e-CRM literature investigates e-CRM activities relating to service quality from the perspective of enterprises. These studies seek to identify the factors involved in customer satisfaction, loyalty, and trust, as well as the resources and technology required to achieve them. Several researches also focused on the significance of service experience[3] and examined CRM implementation strategies.[4] Therefore, we consider experience with e-service a critical aspect of e-CRM, and focus on the means by which customer needs can be satisfied and customers retained through the implementation of appropriate e-CRM services.

Before revising business strategy, companies need to completely recognize customer expectations and examine the difference between expectations and perceptions. In this chapter, we aim to revisit the value of e-services based on customer usage and propose a customer value framework connecting customer needs with CRM e-services. The goal is to assist companies in their quest to enhance customer satisfaction and loyalty with respect to e-CRM issues.

A New CRM Framework

Customer value can be classified into four categories: self-actualized value, social and emotional value, added value, and functional value.[5] The lowest level of customer value is concrete and the highest level of customer value is abstract. All levels of customer value are interconnected, and higher levels of customer value need to be satisfied from lower levels of customer value. This chapter proposes a customer value framework based on two dimensions: customer value and e-CRM processes.

In Table 5.1, the two lowest levels of customer value are functional and added value, which encompass the concept of CRM 1.0. Only closed or one-way communication is allowed in CRM 1.0, indicating that only firms could decide when to communicate with customers. At this level, customers desire useful e-services with basic functions and a few extended e-services to obtain added value. For example, customers need Google to help them to search for information and guide them to related websites. These two levels of customer value are based on basic and expected value. Companies must provide e-services that customers perceive as useful and endeavor to fulfill the needs of their customers.

The third level of value is social and emotional. These are emphasized in CRM 2.0, in which value cocreation is a two-way interaction. At this level, companies provide e-services to fulfill the value desired by customers and enhance the sense of belonging perceived by customers, and the influence of word-of-mouth is most noticeable at this level. The satisfaction resulting from delivering social and emotional value is the most important for the creation and retention of customers. The highest level of value is self-actualized, which is also expected by customers. At this level, customers expect pleasant surprises from the companies they deal with. This concept is promoted in CRM 3.0, wherein customers are encouraged to solve problems on their own as well as provide suggestions and comments to improve the e-services, thereby enhancing their sustainability. Customers provide enterprises with valuable information, based on the concept of customer-centric radiation. At this level, customers dominate the process of CRM, helping companies to retain customers and increase profits.

Prediction of Customer Value

We employ a Markov chain to predict the level of customer value using Bayesian theory to forecast appropriate CRM e-services. A Markov chain is a sequence of random variables, which assumes that the present state, future state, and past states are independent. Markov chains are described by direct graphs where the edges between two states are labeled by probabilities. Theoretically, Markov chains are used for the prediction of interrelated states (events) based on time. The major advantage of Markov chains is that the current state may assist in predicting the following state. In this work, the level of customer value changes sequentially through each of the levels. Our approach identifies the lower level of customer value must be addressed before progressing to higher levels of customer value. Hence, this research utilizes Markov chain to predict the future level of customer value (i.e., four states including functional value, added value, social and emotional value, and self-actualized value).

Markov chains have been applied in many fields, such as medicine, geography, finance, sports, entertainment, and business. In this research, we assumed that the four states were four levels of customer value: self-actualized value, social and emotional value, added value, and functional value. Moreover, we provided three indicators to evaluate the performance and accuracy of the Markov chain approach: precision, recall, and

Table 5.1 A new CRM framework

Concept		Pre-sale	Transaction		Post-sale
Process for creating customer value		Acquire	Use	Feedback	Retain
Process for creating business value		Marketing	Sale	Post-service	Revise
Lerel of customer value		Attract	\<— CRME-service process —\> Interact		Retain
Surprise from customers (CRM 3.0 concept: Self-problem solving and self-control)	Self-actualized value (Unexpected value)	Products and services provide self-actualized value	Customer-centric radiation B ⟷ C ⟷ (radiating)		Customer domination
Comprehensiveness from customers (CRM 1.0 concept: e-service standard)	Social and emotional value (Desired value)	Products and services provide belongingness	Two-way interaction B ⟷ C		Social and emotional satisfaction
Satisfaction from customers (CRM 2.0 concept: value co-creation from social network)	Added value (Expectant value)	Products and services are comprehensive	One-way communication B ⟶ C		Completeness
Usefulness from customers (CRM 1.0 concept: Basic functions of e-services)	Functional value (Basic value)	Products and services provide functional value	Closed B C		Perceived usefulness

F-measure. Evaluation indices, such as precision, recall, and F-measure, are widely used in the domain of information retrieval. Precision is defined as the proportion of predictions and ideal needs ascribed to each (Eq. 5.1). By considering only the top most results returned by a system, precision takes into account all predicted needs above a particular threshold of significance. Recall is defined as the proportion of ideal needs predicted out of all ideal needs available (Eq. 5.2). It is trivial to achieve 100% recall by fulfilling all needs in response to a given point in time. That is, recall alone is insufficient; one needs to measure the number of irrelevant predicted needs. F-measure is the weighted harmonic mean of precision and recall (Eq. 5.3). A traditional F-measure or balanced F-score is also known as the F-measure, in which recall and precision are evenly weighted. Hence, this research aims to utilize three indicators to measure the performance of Markov chains in terms of adequacy:

$$\text{Precision} = \frac{\text{Predicted and ideal value}}{\text{All value predicted}} \quad (5.1)$$

$$\text{Recall} = \frac{\text{Predicted and ideal value}}{\text{Out of all ideal value available}} \quad (5.2)$$

$$\text{F-measure} = \frac{2 \times \text{Precision} \times \text{Recall}}{\text{Precision} + \text{Recall}} \quad (5.3)$$

Bayesian probability models are used to forecast posterior probability according to prior probability and sample probability, in which all events are interrelated. Bayesian inference is an approach using statistical inferences. The probabilities can be adjusted when new evidence occurs. Bayesian probability model determines what one's probability for the hypothesis is based on the known outcomes. The advantage of this approach is the ability to infer outcomes despite small sample sizes and limited information. The Bayesian theorem specifies how to use new information to adjust estimated probability, and the basic assumption is that all variables are independent (e.g., $P(A \cap B) = P(A) \times P(B)$). We assumed three CRM e-services (attraction, interaction, and retention) as dependent events, and each level of customer value could provide a combination of CRM e-services. The reason for this was that, in practice, each process of e-service operates independently. No doubt, each user uses a particular combination of CRM e-services, and Bayesian theory is used to estimate the highest number of conditional probability for all CRM e-service combinations for each user. We also used adequacy to measure the performance of the Bayesian theory. Adequacy is defined as the percentage of predicted e-services that are actually used (Eq. 5.4) For instance, if our approach provided a combination A1, I2, and R3 and the actual usage of combination is A1, I3, and R3, the percentage of adequacy would be 66.7%:

$$\text{Adequacy} = \frac{\text{Actual usage of e-services}}{\text{All predicted e-services}} \qquad (5.4)$$

A Real-World Example for Illustration

We selected iTunes in Taiwan as the e-service platform for our case study due to the sufficiently high number of users and the variety of e-services it provides. iTunes is a well-known and popular platform for users to download music, movies, TV programs, podcasts, and other applications. We applied the proposed value framework to e-services from iTunes. In Table 5.2, iTunes e-services are matched according to the four levels of customer value (functional value (B), added value (C), social and emotional value (E), self-actualized value (S), and three types of CRM processes (attraction, interaction, and retention). We attempted to match 29 iTunes e-services with our framework. In the category of attract, e-services are intended to attract users. In the category of interact, e-services can assist users in interacting with iTunes. In the category of retain, e-services can provide increased benefit to promote or maintain loyalty. The proposed value framework covers 18 e-services of attraction, five e-services of interaction, and six e-services of retention. In order to reduce complexity, we assumed each e-service only belonged to one category, although a number of e-services may be classified in more than one category. We attempted to match them to the most reasonable and appropriate category.

We interviewed 30 iTunes users (15 students and 15 workers) with the experience of using iTunes services and collected information on their behavior. We discovered that students and workers are distinct with regard to paying for iTunes services and user preferences. We used economic

Table 5.2 iTunes e-services matched with the proposed framework

	Attract	**Interact**	**Retain**
S	AS_1: Customized Music Recommendation AS_2: Personalized Music Composition AS_3: Customized Content and Delivery	IS_1: Music/ Application Evaluation	RS_1: Personalized Music Channel Management
E	AE_1: Music Usage from other Peers in the Community AE_2: iTunes Gift Card Delivery AE_3: Online Sharing	IE_1: Online Forum	RE_1: Music Recommendation from Good Peers RE_2: Comments Sharing for Music
C	AC_1: Radio or TV programs Subscription AC_2: iPod Games AC_3: iTunes Scholar Videos AC_4: Applications AC_5: Movies or Videos AC_6: Bundling Service	IC_1: iTalk Online Customer Service IC_2: Email Service	RC_1: New Product and Information via Email RC_2: Application Update
B	AB_1: Music Update and Download (each week) AB_2: Free Trial Music (each week) AB_3: Music Recording Service	IB_1: Self-Service (FAQ)	RB_1: Discount Provision

Source: (Summarized by this book)

Table 5.3. iTunes user type

		Economic ability	
		Low	**High**
Involvement of music	**Heavy**	Addicted student	Addicted worker
	Light	Typical student	Typical worker

means and involvement in music to segment the 30 users according to four types. As shown in Table 5.3, study participants were divided into addicted students (7), typical students (8), addicted workers (6), and typical workers (9).

The behavior of users using the iTunes services varied according to interview results. We consider light involvement in music as a feature of typical users and heavy involvement of music as a feature of addicted users. Limited economic means could result in a limited budget to pay for iTunes services. In contrast, strong economic means may facilitate the usage of iTunes services. Typical students spent less on iTunes services due to monetary concerns and low music involvement and tended to find opportunities to obtain free videos and applications. Addicted students were interested in information related to music, entertainment, and learning services, as well as interacting with peers. However, their spending was limited to e-services. Typical workers considered music a leisure media and paid for music and entertainment products. Addicted workers had a passion for music and were economically stable. They were particularly interested in information about music or products and demanded high quality e-services and customization.

In addition to customer segmentation, we collected information on e-service usage through interviews. We asked participants to provide information regarding e-service usage in the previous 13 days (around two weeks). Based on this information, we attempted to match each used e-service with a category of customer value at a level of CRM process. We also requested the users to provide information concerning at least one e-service they used each day. In this manner, we integrated the e-services used by each type of user to simulate a chain. Due to difficulties in obtaining data concerning long-term e-service usage, we assumed that the usage was routinely repeated over time. In other words, we extended the simulated samples to 26, 39, 52, and 65 days based on 13 days of e-service usage.

Mining Demanded Customer Services

We simulated 26, 39, 52, and 65 days of usage for each type of user. Based on the e-service usage we collected, we assumed that each day represented a level of customer value. In other words, each customer used several e-services to fulfill a level of customer value each day. Two-thirds of the data was utilized for building the transition matrix and one-third of the data was employed for verifying validity based on the constructed transition matrix. Indicators for validity were precision, recall, and F-measure. The results of the simulation revealed that 52 days had the best outcome with regard to precision, recall, and F-measure. In particular, precision rates were 70.59% for the typical student and addicted worker, 64.71% for the addicted student, and 50% for the typical worker. The average precision rate percentage was 64.7%. The recall rate was 66.7% for the typical student, 69.57% for the addicted student, 57.41% for the typical worker, and 78.26% for the addicted worker. The average recall rate percentage was 61.48%. The F-measure for 52 days was 67.91%, which was the best value among all simulated data.

Our results also revealed that the precision rate was high for typical students and addicted workers, reaching 60% to 70% for the various periods of time simulated in the study. Typical students had the highest degree of involvement with music, while addicted workers had the lowest. The precision rates were different before the five predicted days, and close in the long term for the four types. Meanwhile, the precision rate for typical workers was the lowest. The average precision rate for data was 59.38% (26), 62.52% (39), 64.70% (52), and 59.52% (65). The trend revealed that precision rates increased as duration increased to 52 days, but decreased beyond 52 days. The reason for this was that the transition matrix stabilized as the amount of data increased, and predicted customer value may be the same in the long term. However, actual customer value may still change periodically. Consequently, the best outcome of the experimental simulations was 52 days.

The result of recall rate for all data was 57.5% (26 days), 62.5% (39 days), 71.97% (52 days), and 61.84% (65 days). The coverage of the predicted customer value was the highest when the data was extended to simulate 52 days. The trend also revealed that the number of days and precision and recall are inversely proportional (Table 5.4). In addition, recall rates were close among the four types of users as shown in Figure 1.2. The recall rate for addicted workers was superior to that of the other three types of participants after 9 days. Finally, the F-measure for all data was 3.11% (26 days), 60.71% (39 days), 67.91% (52 days), and 58.20% (65 days). This also indicated that the ability to predict customer value for typical students and addicted workers was the best, and the typical worker was the worst with the number of days set to 52. The F-measure value for addicted students was in between.

We also employed *adequacy* as an indicator for measuring the effectiveness of the Bayesian approach. We collected data of 13 days of e-service

Table 5.4 Performance of Markow chain from simulation

	Precision			Recall		F-measure		
	Best	Worst	Average		Average	Best	Worst	
26 days	Typical student (62.5%) Addicted student (62.5%) Addicted worker (62.5%)	Typical worker (50%)	59.38%	57.5%	53.11%	Addicted worker	Typical worker	
39 days	Typical student (66.67%) Addicted Student (66.67%) Addicted worker (66.67%)	Typical worker (50%)	62.52%	62.5%	60.71%	Typical student Addicted worker	Typical worker	
52 days	Typical student (70.59%) Addicted worker (70.59%)	Typical worker (52.94%)	64.70%	71.97%	67.91%	Addicted worker	Typical worker	
65 days	Typical student (66.67%)	Typical worker (47.62%)	59.52%	61.84%	58.20%	Typical student	Typical worker	

usage from interviews. After identifying the level of customer value, we forecast the most appropriate combination of e-services. We assumed that each customer used a combination of CRM e-services each day, including services related to attraction, interaction, and retention. However, it was not necessary for a user to utilize all three types of e-services each day. Therefore, we extended the 13-day model to simulate 26, 39, 52, and 65 days for each type of user. We utilized two-thirds of the days to build the model and one-third of the days to verify validity. We employed *adequacy* as the indicator of validity pertaining to the Bayesian approach. The average degree of adequacy for all numbers of days and all types of users are shown in Table 5.5.

In Table 5.5, the average degree of adequacy for levels B (81.6%) and C (89%) was approximately 80% for the typical student. This number was representative of the recommended CRM e-services matching customer value. As for addicted students, the average degree of adequacy for levels C and E was between 80% and 90%, and only the adequacy number for level B was low (approximately 75%). The average degree of adequacy for levels B and C for the typical worker was between 70% and 85%. The average degree of adequacy for level E (around 75%) was lower than levels B and C. This result was not representative of level S due to an insufficient (one sample) number of days. The reason for this was that this type of user merely uses e-services to satisfy value (needs) from level S. As for addicted workers, the average degree of adequacy for level E was between 70% and 80% and for level S was between 80% and 90%. The average degree of adequacy for level C was low (around 50%), and the reason may be that users use e-services mostly from higher levels (E and S). Level B was not representative either was due to an insufficient number of days required for verification, because this type of user merely uses e-services to satisfy value (needs) from level B.

Mining CRM Services

In this chapter, we proposed a holistic customer value framework using a Markov chain and Bayesian probability model to predict customer value (step 1) and deliver an appropriate combination of CRM e-services (step 2). In step 1, 52 days provided the best prediction performance;

Table 5.5 Average degree of adequacy for various types of users over various periods of time

Data	Adequacy																			
	Typical student			Addicted student				Typical worker					Addicted worker				
	B	C		B	C	E	B	C	E	S		B	C	E	S
26	0.734	0.833		0.723	0.667	0.753	0.792	1	0.667	1			0.225	0.778	0.89
39	0.816	0.793		0.734	0.835	0.835	0.778	0.793	0.667	1		1	0.558	0.736	0.906
52	0.793	0.89		0.778	0.89	0.835	0.76	0.834	0.667	1		1	0.505	0.667	0.752
65	0.787	0.81		0.730	0.89	0.802	0.784	0.862	0.89	1		1	0.604	0.81	0.918

however, performance was reduced when the modeled period was increased beyond that point. The reason was that the Markov chain converges in the long term and may predict the same outcome and results with decreasing accuracy. The results also revealed that 52 days was the optimal data size in terms of precision, recall, and F-measure. Our results also showed that precision and recall were trade-offs. F-measure was also superior at 52 days, particularly for addicted students and addicted workers. Thus, enterprises must optimize data size to avoid a stabilized transition matrix, which in this case means that firms would have to collect two months of data (to match the 52 days in the study) as the basis for prediction.

In step 2, the results revealed that 52 days was optimal for typical students and addicted students. In addition, the optimal period of study for typical workers and addicted workers was 65 days. This means that enterprises would have to collect more data to predict the behavior of typical and addicted workers. In particular, the performance of the Bayesian probability model increased with an increase in the length of the study period. In summary, this research used a two-step prediction for customer value and CRM e-service combinations. Simulation results revealed that the number of days should be large enough to improve performance. That is, the data should be no less than 52 days (i.e., 2 months) for either the Markov chain or the Bayesian theorem. Segmentation of customers could also help firms to identify customer characteristics and discover how to deal with their needs.

In this chapter, the concept of service mining provides a new viewpoint to reexamine CRM on electronic services. Customer behavior is difficult to predict especially on Internet. Thus, service mining can help firms to simplify customer behavior on services and predict potential services in advance. Human beings always repeat 80% of behavior according to psychology. That is, enterprises may identify key successful and most used services by modeling the behavior on services. The service will be refined and reorganized to earn more benefit and profit.

CHAPTER 6

Discovering Service Failure and Recovery

This chapter provides a method to discover the casual effect among service failure, service recovery, and trust. The method used to analyze casual effect is system dynamics. This chapter covers the method (technology), scope (service recovery management), and domain (electronic service) as given in Figure 1.3. In this chapter, service mining is used to assist enterprises to reexamine the factors that affect service failure and how to recover efficiently.

In modern societies, the speed and convenience of Internet contribute greatly to the development and growth of e-commerce. A competitive e-commerce environment with low switching costs would result in a high customer churn rate on the Internet. A research report showed an average of 25% annual churn rate for Internet Service Providers.[1] To increase the customer retention rate and consequently the revenue and profit, firms often provide online services (e-services) as a critical ingredient. Increasing the customer retention rate by just 5% can boost profits by 25% to 85%.[2]

Trust is a fundamental element in establishing and maintaining long-term relationships between firms and customers.[3] The lack of online interpersonal interaction and the absence of physical contact in online exchanges have strengthened the significance of e-trust.[4] Trust is the critical component driving customer satisfaction, loyalty, and purchase intention in online services.[5] Hence, the importance of trust cannot be overemphasized and it is always crucial for firms to gain customer trust based on online service applications.

Firms inevitably experience service failure. For example, the B2B online news (2010) announced that "Amazon Has Suffered a Temporary Web Service Failure" during the Christmas season, which caused troubles for consumers buying presents. A similar headline in *The Epoch Times* (2011) reported that "Bank of America Website Down, Leaving Customers Unhappy." In this case, a cracked website was too slow to load, which made customers unable to navigate and they stopped their online banking.[6] Such failures definitely decrease customer trust in service providers and increase their dissatisfaction. The cost of acquiring and serving new customers is five times greater than the cost of retaining and satisfying current customers.[7] Service recovery, however, is a subtle issue for firms. The "recovery paradox" literature indicates that customers who have experienced service failure but ultimately have their problems solved will become much more loyal than those who do not encounter failures. Trust is a key mediator in the process of service recovery.[8] Trust can be influenced by an outstanding recovery performance and subsequently enhance customer loyalty. High service recovery can positively affect customer satisfaction, purchase intention, and positive word of mouth.[9] These again indicate the essential role of trust in service environments.

Although many studies examine traditional service recovery, relatively few discuss service recovery in e-commerce. The critical distinctions between traditional services and e-services include reduced human interaction and the mediating role of technology.[10] Consequently, the recovery difficulties and the factors influencing the recovery process online differ from those in offline circumstances. In addition, most researchers who have highlighted the significant mediating role of trustworthiness in the recovery process used quantitative methods to analyze the linear relationship between variables and service recovery.

This chapter proposes a system dynamics approach to discovering the causal relationships between trust and a number of variables in an e-service recovery process. "System dynamics is a perspective and set of conceptual tools that enable us to understand the structure and dynamics of complex systems."[11] Using the system dynamics approach, we can explicitly observe how things influence each other under complex systems over time, which allows firms to create more effective service recovery strategies. In this chapter, the goal is to explore whether e-service recovery help enhance the trust of customers who experience service failure and what are the major factors influencing e-service recovery in terms of e-trust.

A Holistic Model of System Dynamics

System dynamics, first proposed by Jay W. Forrester in mid-1950s, is an approach to dealing with "internal feedback loops" and "time delays" that affect the behaviors among complex systems over time. This approach can help researchers gain insight into the dynamic changes existing in every human activity and improve awareness of the complex phenomena in the real world. System dynamics can simulate considerable perspectives and provide long-term solutions because it effectively copes with the dynamic changes, feedback information, and time delays in complex environments. System dynamics consists of causal relationships and utilizes feedback systems as the basis of causal feedback loops. Additionally, researchers can define the problems through the use of causal relationships. As a result, complex problems can be presented in a concise and systematic way to help managers to obtain a clearer view.

The first step in modeling a complex process in a system is to discover the casual relationships among the variables. This chapter attempts to design the process of e-service recovery based on previous research studies. Service recovery process can be divided into three phases: prerecovery, immediate recovery, and follow-up recovery phases.[12] The failure severity, customer loyalty, perceived preservice quality, and company guarantees all affect customer expectations of service recovery in the prerecovery phase. The role of customer expectation is critical to the success of service recovery. If firms have a superior understanding of customer expectations, they can easily implement an effective recovery strategy to exceed customer expectations. Then, in the immediate recovery phase, there are four key elements to a successful recovery: the types of recovery activity (psychological and tangible efforts) and the delivery of service recovery (speed of recovery and frontline empowerment). When failures occur, firms must quickly respond to customers, endeavor to appease them, and treat them fairly. Finally, follow-up recovery, which involves an apology or a tangible token, can strengthen the effectiveness of recovery and subsequently lead to the success of maintaining long-term customer loyalty and satisfaction. Figure 6.1 demonstrates the proposed causal loop diagram.

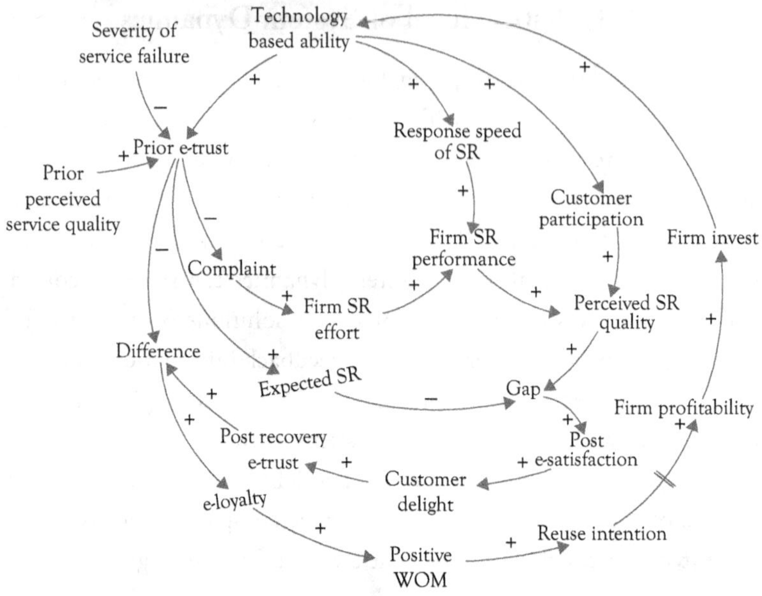

Figure 6.1 Causal loop diagram

A Simulation Analysis

The four diagrams in Figure 6.2 illustrate the process of e-service recovery in terms of e-trust. The simulation time is 12 months to evaluate a long-term performance of e-services recovery, as firms typically measure their profitability annually. Figure 6.2(a) indicates that customer's prior e-trust will decrease in the first month due to the occurrence of service failures. Simultaneously, firm profits fall to the lowest point. When firms perceive their declined business, they will endeavor to recover customers in the second month. Accordingly, customer's post e-trust gradually rises and increases 6% in the sixth month (Figure 6.2(b)). Though firms improve their profit slightly after recovery, they are still below the starting point (initial value = 50) from the first to the ninth month. This implies that there are time delays between customer reuse intention and firm profitability. When customers perceive the recovery performance and reestablish their e-trust on service providers, they may reuse the service after a period to test the inconsistence between their reaction and perception. Hence, there is a sharp increase on firm profitability in the 10th month (Figure 6.2(c)). On the other hand, technology-based ability plays an important role in

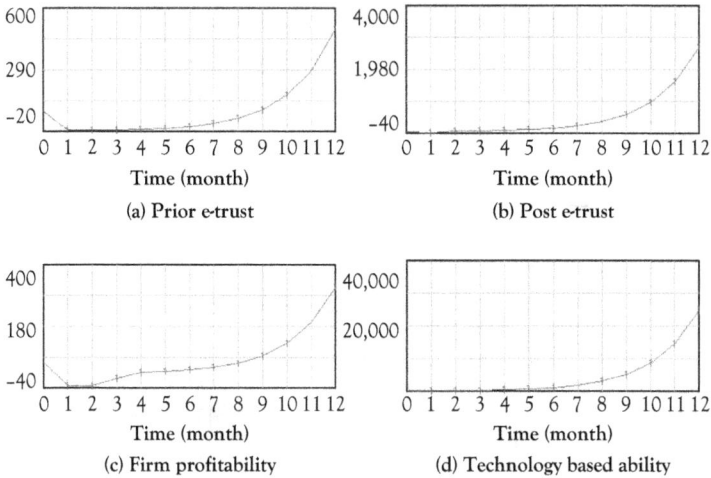

Figure 6.2 The results of simulation for four stock variables

the recovery process (Figure 6.2(d)). The higher technological ability a firm possesses, the more effective recovery it will perform on customer e-trust. In summary, service recovery seems to cost firms in the short run, and while recovery effects are difficult to detect, it can boost the firms' profits and revenue in the long run.

Prior Perceived Service Quality

When the level of failure severity is the same (IV: 80), two groups of customers perceive two different levels of service quality before recovery. The first group has low perceived service quality (IV: 20), while the second group has high perceived service quality (IV: 80). Figure 6.3(a) indicates that the second group has greater prior e-trust than the first group when failures happen in the first month. That is, customer-perceived service quality has positive effects on customer's prior e-trust. However, the results of Figure 6.3(b) reveal that the post e-trust in the first group grows faster than that in the second group during recovery. Additionally, firm profitability in the first group increases faster and becomes higher than the second group (Figure 6.3(c)). Although two lines of profitability seem to converge in the long run, the gap between the two groups can lead to a range of 0.04 to 3.5 times difference in profitability every month. This

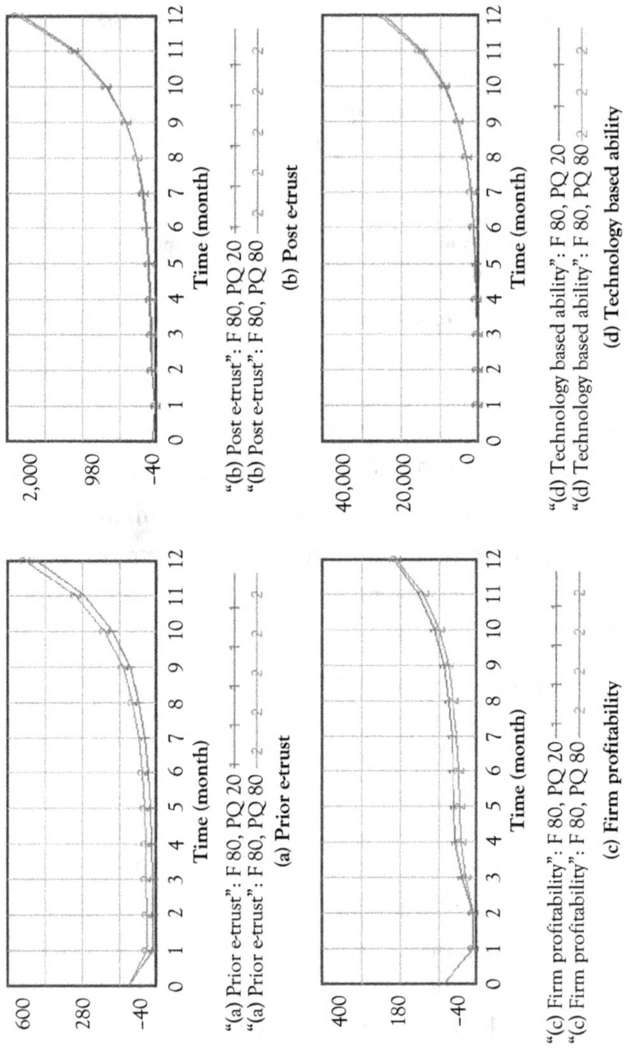
600
280
-40
0 1 2 3 4 5 6 7 8 9 10 11 12
Time (month)
"(a) Prior e-trust" : F 80, PQ 20
"(a) Prior e-trust" : F 80, PQ 80
(a) Prior e-trust
2,000
980
-40
0 1 2 3 4 5 6 7 8 9 10 11 12
Time (month)
"(b) Post e-trust" : F 80, PQ 20
"(b) Post e-trust" : F 80, PQ 80
(b) Post e-trust
400
180
-40
0 1 2 3 4 5 6 7 8 9 10 11 12
Time (month)
"(c) Firm profitability": F 80, PQ 20
"(c) Firm profitability": F 80, PQ 80
(c) Firm profitability
40,000
20,000
0
0 1 2 3 4 5 6 7 8 9 10 11 12
Time (month)
"(d) Technology based ability": F 80, PQ 20
"(d) Technology based ability": F 80, PQ 80
(d) Technology based ability

Figure 6.3 The results for different levels of prior perceived service quality

implies that customers with high prior service experience can expect high service recovery. When firms do not reach or exceed their expectations, customers may not feel satisfied with service recovery. This results in a reduction of customer reuse intention and the slow growth of profits for firms. On the other hand, Figure 6.5(d) shows that there is not much difference in technology-based ability under the two levels of prior perceived service quality. It reveals the same trend as we observe in Figure 6.4(d) that the higher technological ability a firm possesses, the more effective recovery it will lead to. In summary, customers who initially have a low prior perceived service quality will generate more profit for firms than those with high perceived quality after recovery.

Failure Severity

When the prior perceived service quality of customers is similar (IV: 50), the occurrence of failures with high (IV: 80) and low (IV: 20) severity will have different effects on e-recovery performance. Figure 6.4(a) indicates that failure severity negatively affects customer's prior e-trust. That is, customers who encounter a low degree of failure have greater e-trust than those encountering a high degree of failure. However, Figure 6.4(b) indicates that customers with high failure severity will possess higher post e-trust than the others after service recovery. Figure 6.4(c) shows that customers with high failure severity are 0.05 to 2.8 times more profitable every month than customers with a low degree of failure. Customers who initially encountered high degree of service failures but finally had their problems solved would generate greater profit for the firm than those with low failure severity. This implies that customers with high failure severity may strongly voice their complaints; the more they speak out, the more recovery efforts firms will make. Simultaneously, customers with high failure severity are more willing to engage in recovery. The more efforts the customers contribute, the higher the recovery performance. On the other hand, Figure 6.4(d) shows that there is not much difference in technology-based ability under the two levels of failure severity. In brief, customers who have experienced high failure severity and finally have their problems solved have higher reuse intention and thus generate more profit for the firm than those experiencing a low degree of failure.

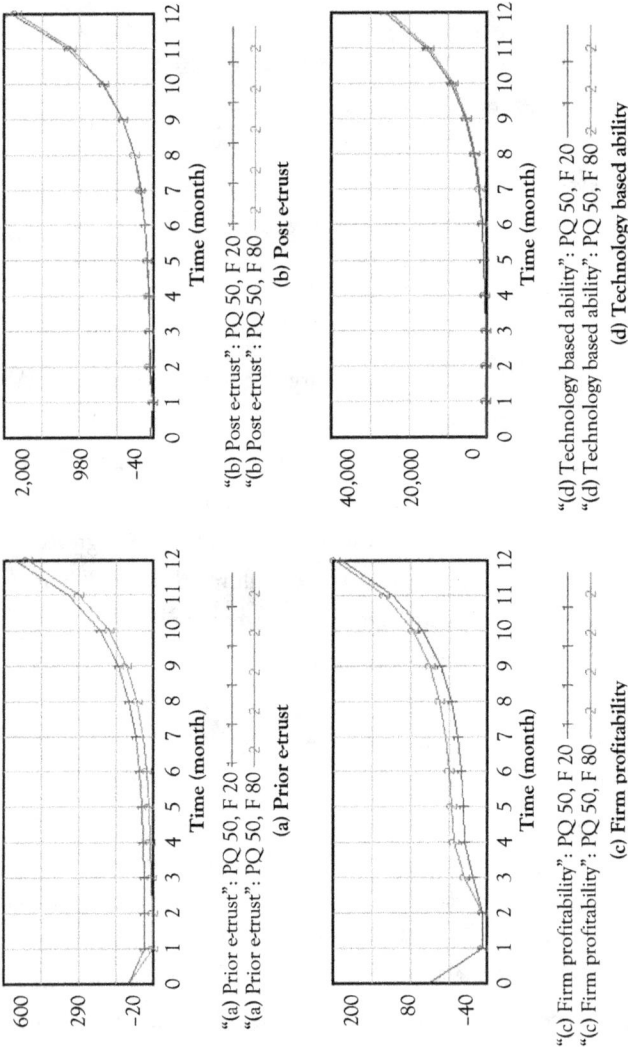

Figure 6.4 *The results for different levels of severity of failure*

Customer Participation

Since customers play a key role in the e-recovery process, the degree of their participation will affect the recovery performance. This study considers three groups of customers who encounter the same failure severity (IV: 80) and possess identical prior perceived service quality (IV: 80), but contribute 20%, 50%, and 80% efforts to self recovery. As Figure 6.5(a) shows, the curves of prior e-trust in three groups appear similar before firms rectify their problems. However, Figure 6.5(b) reveals that the more customers engage in recovery process, the higher their e-trust will be. There is not much difference in the three curves before the seventh month, but the gaps widen in the eighth month. The change of post e-trust in these three groups significantly affects firm profitability. Figure 6.5(c) shows that the amount of firms' profits suddenly falls to the lowest point due to the occurrence of failures in the beginning. Next, a time delay obviously exists in the first and the second month, followed by a slight increase in firm profitability from the third to the seventh months. The gap appearing between the three curves becomes larger over time. This suggests that reduced interpersonal interaction and mediating technology result in high recovery difficulties in electronic commerce. When failures occur, customers rarely seek aid from the first-line staff members of e-service companies. Customer also causes some e-failures, such as missing passwords. If customers perceive the risks of failures, they may be unwilling to participate in self-recovery because of the fear of jeopardizing their safety and property. An example of this is theft identity to be used in illegal actions. While customer participation can help speed up the recovery process and shorten the recovery time, it can also result in high recovery performance. On the other hand, customers who engage in the self-recovery process may have a better understanding of the e-service or have more interaction with service providers via website or e-mail. Figure 6.5(d) shows little difference between the three groups in terms of technological ability. That is, the ratio that firms invest in technology is the same regardless of how profitable they are. This implies that firms may have grasped the appropriate ratio of investment that has the greatest effectiveness in self-service recovery technologies. In summary, customers

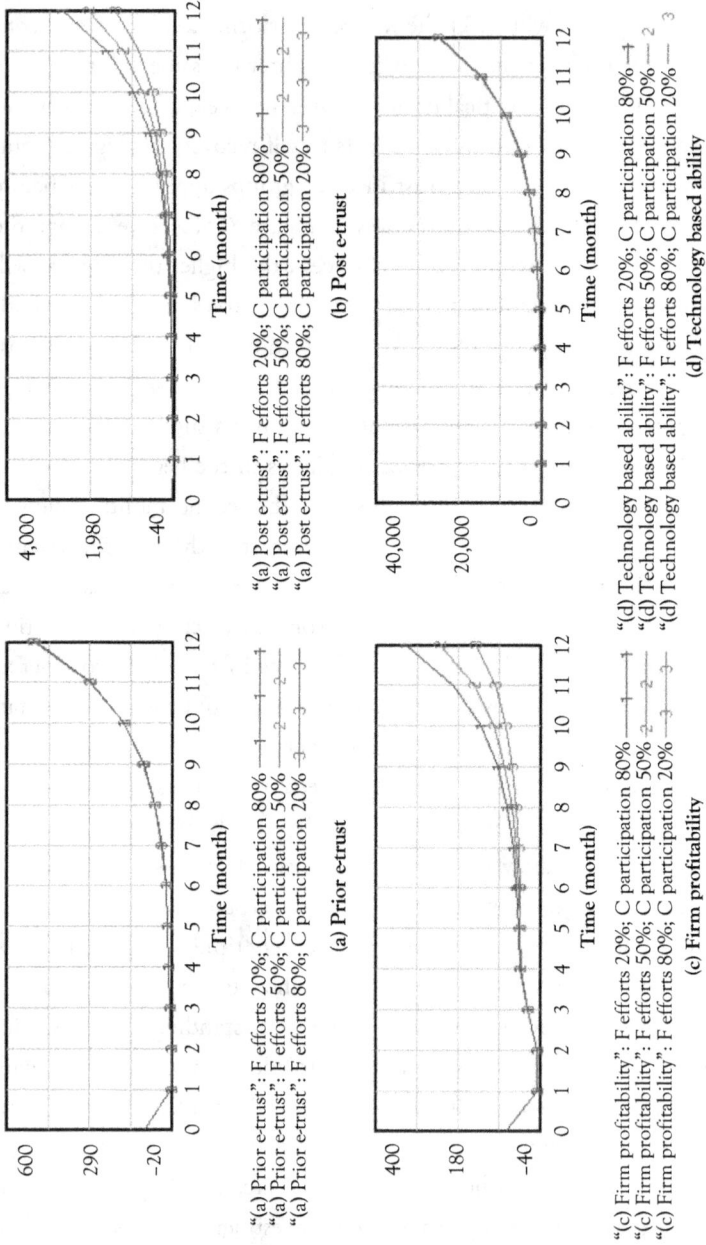

"(a) Prior e-trust": F efforts 20%; C participation 80% ——1——
"(a) Prior e-trust": F efforts 50%; C participation 50% ——2——
"(a) Prior e-trust": F efforts 80%; C participation 20% ——3——

(a) Prior e-trust

"(a) Post e-trust": F efforts 20%; C participation 80% ——1——
"(a) Post e-trust": F efforts 50%; C participation 50% ——2——
"(a) Post e-trust": F efforts 80%; C participation 20% ——3——

(b) Post e-trust

"(c) Firm profitability": F efforts 20%; C participation 80% ——1——
"(c) Firm profitability": F efforts 50%; C participation 50% ——2——
"(c) Firm profitability": F efforts 80%; C participation 20% ——3——

(c) Firm profitability

"(d) Technology based ability": F efforts 20%; C participation 80% ——1——
"(d) Technology based ability": F efforts 50%; C participation 50% ——2——
"(d) Technology based ability": F efforts 80%; C participation 20% ——3——

(d) Technology based ability

Figure 6.5 The results for different degrees of customer participation

with high participation are critical to successful recovery and can also generate more profit for firms.

The Value of Service Recovery

E-service in the fiercely competitive e-commerce has become more and more important over the years and thus has drawn a lot of research attention. To maintain long-term relationships with customers and their reuse intention rate, service providers must satisfy the needs of customers, especially when service failures occur. If firms cannot deal with failures effectively, customers may easily become upset and quickly change their service providers. One the other hand, e-trust also plays a critical role in driving customer relationships in the e-recovery process. Thus, service managers must thoroughly consider the recovery process when designing an efficient and successful strategy.

This chapter employs a system dynamics approach to modeling an e-service recovery framework incorporated with e-trust and providing firms with insights into the causal relationships among trust issues in the complex recovery process. This chapter observes that e-service recovery will enhance the trust of customers when facing service failure. However, this relationship will be contingent upon such factors as firm's technological ability, customers' prior perceived service quality, severity of failures, and customer participation.

The analytic results show that a firm's technology-based ability will contribute to effective recovery and thus gain customer e-trust. Customers' prior perceived service quality positively affects prior recovery e-trust when failures occur. However, customers who posses low perceived service quality will generate more profit for firms than those with a high perceived service quality. The severity of failures negatively influences customer's prior recovery e-trust. Customers who encounter high failure severity yet ultimately resolve their problems will generate more profit for firms than those with a low degree of service failure. Finally, customer participation is also critical to the success of e-recovery. The more customers contribute to the recovery process, the higher post e-trust will be.

In this chapter, the concept of service mining provides a novel viewpoint to look at service failure and recovery by using system dynamics. It also provides a macro view of a holistic framework in a complex environment. The discovered factors also help companies identify critical factors in the integrated framework by simulation. Compared to existing researches, system dynamics in service mining can help enterprises discover more factors and provides a long-term simulation to observe the results of service recovery.

CHAPTER 7

Mining Service Brands

This chapter provides an insight on how customers perceived a service brand by collecting information on what they used for dress in the service environment. The method to analyze apparel of clothing is genetic algorithm. This chapter covers the method (technology), scope (service brand management), and domain (service in the restaurant) as given in Figure 1.3. In this chapter, service mining is used to assist enterprises better understand what customers perceived of a service brand in terms of apparel.

The rapid growth of the service industry has drawn managerial and scholarly attention to the significance of service branding in the field of marketing. A service brand helps consumers reduce search costs, simplify purchase decisions, and diminish perceived risk of service usage and allow consumers projecting their self-image, thereby reflecting values or characteristics that differ from others.[1]

In particular, prior studies have shown the influence of image on customer postpurchase behavior. A good brand image enhances overall customer experience and arouses customer satisfaction, loyalty, and commitment to the service provider in mobile phone sector.[2] The results showed the significant effect of brand image on brand equity, which affects the customer's brand preference.[3] Other studies have also shown the important role of brand image in mediating customer behavior such as user brand loyalty, perceived service quality, brand personality, and customer experience with service.[4]

Based on the significance of service branding and customer perception, we contend that marketers should focus more attention on how customers perceive a brand image than how the brand image is delivered to customers. However, research available on the association between customer behavior and service branding is scant. Prior literature shows clothing to be a form of nonverbal communication and helps people communicate with others easily and smoothly on social occasions.[5] Other studies have suggested that service organizations can leverage the importance of clothing in delivering a brand signal.[6] In this chapter, we examine the relationship between customer clothing preference and influential factors on service brand image by developing a literature-based conceptual model. Symbolic interactionism indicates that people attribute symbolic meaning to clothing and dress based on those symbolic meanings; thus, we expect that customers with different clothing preferences possess dissimilar images of a service brand. Finally, we use a genetic algorithm approach to discover the optimal service brand from customer clothing preferences. If customer apparel preference shows a favorable service brand and service brand image, it can provide cues for frontline staff to satisfy and meet customer expectations in service delivery.

Service Brand Model

Drawing on prior literature, this study develops a conceptual model, as shown in Figure 7.1. In this model, we focus on the level of fitness between the service brand and customer clothing apparel. For a service brand, we consider that service brand personality and service experiences are important elements, as highlighted in previous studies.[7]

"Brand personality" is "the set of human characteristics associated with a brand" and a brand personality scale (BPS) has been developed accordingly.[8] However, the BPS has been criticized as unsuitable for the service industries. The modified Aaker's BPS was conducted to an empirical study based on the scenario of restaurant industries.[9] The modified BPS was applied to restaurant industries (Table 7.1). In this chapter, we adopt this modified model for the following reason. The past research

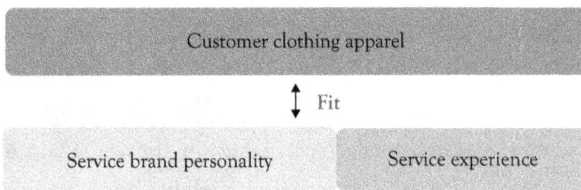

Figure 7.1 Service brand model

Table 7.1 Modified brand personality scale

Competence	Sincerity	Excitement	Sophistication
Reliable	Honest	Trendy	Upper-class
Corporate	Sincere	Unique	Glamorous
Successful	Real	Up-to-date	Charming
Leader	Wholesome		
Confident	Original		
	Cheerful		
	Friendly		

Source: Musante et al., (2008).

focuses on how brand personality influences consumer postconsumption behavior such as customer satisfaction, loyalty, and commitment toward a brand. Researchers investigating the relationship between service brand image and brand personality are scant. Second, we believe this model allows us to evaluate customer images of a service brand and in establishing an optimal service brand.

Furthermore, a research examined bank customers and the relationship among service experience, feelings, satisfaction, and brand attitudes of these customers.[10] Their research shows that service experience has a significant effect on feelings, satisfaction, and brand attitudes. The findings show three influential elements affecting customer experiences, including core services, employee service, and servicescape. Service experience of satisfied consumers and constructed a hierarchical map showing what elements of the satisfied-customer experience evoke customer feelings and lead to benefits or values (e.g., happiness).[11] The findings show that service experience significantly influences brand meaning. Put together, researchers argue that customer experience can be divided into three categories: core service, servicescape, and employee service.

Clothing refers to any garment worn on the body such as trousers, a dress, and a shirt. Clothing can be a form of nonverbal communication, and has two communication functions. One is "the negotiation of identities." Because clothing is visible to everyone, it helps people negotiate their identity with others. People express themselves and send messages regarding themselves, such as attitude, mood, and status through various types of clothing. The second function clothing serves is "the definition of situations" such as formality, familiarity, and salience[12]. The interrelationships among different situations affect a person's selection of daily clothing.[13] The study results show the interrelationships between temporal clothing functions and clothing orientation factors.

In addition to clothing function, clothing also have symbolic meaning. Symbolic meaning changes with the external environment; people choose appropriate clothing styles that represent themselves (e.g., personal preference and personality) and help them fit into a specific situation. Thus, we concentrate on "the definition of situation" of clothing function and explore the influential situations related to brand image that may affect customer clothing styles in the service context. Service brand personality and service experience can be used to conceptualize the customer imagery of a service brand. The components of service experience (e.g., servicescape or employee uniform) and the influential elements on customer perceptions of brand personality traits (e.g., brand name, slogan, and user imagery) may affect the clothing decisions of customers who believe that appropriate clothing helps them fit into a specific situation and communicate with others. If clothing shows people's imagery of a service brand, this study can use clothing cues to build a favorable customer service brand.

From Apparel to Service Brands

We used a genetic algorithm (GA) approach to predict a service brand image and to build a service brand from consumer perspectives. Before implementing GA, five categories of apparel styles were used based on existing research, including formal, elegant, modern, casual, and sporty. We adopt the fundamental elements of clothing, which include four categories: coat, shirt, skirt, and trousers.[14] Each category has its own attributions, which are mostly adopted from Lin (2007). We also added certain new attributes (e.g., blue jeans and casual jacket). Customers have options on coats, shirts, skirts, and trousers for dressing.

To assess chromosome quality, a fitness function is required to determine the evolution mechanism. A chromosome with a high fitness value represents a higher opportunity to be selected. Conversely, a chromosome with a low fit value is easily eliminated during the evolution process. In this

Service brand personality (18 bits)	Service experience (16 bits)

Chromosome (34 bits)

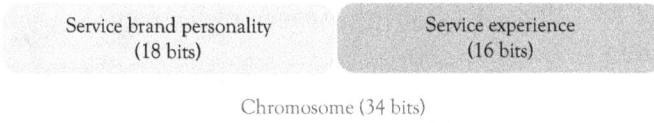

Figure 7.2 Length of a chromosome

study, a chromosome comprises two variables: service brand personality and service experience. The total length of the chromosome is 34 bits, including 18 bits of service brand personality and 16 bits of service experience.

A chromosome theoretically consists of two variables (Figure 7.2). X_i represents the set of attributes of the first variable, service brand personality, and i indicates the number of genes. Service brand personality includes 18 genes, which means that $i = 1, 2, \ldots, 18$. Y_j represents the second variable, service experience, which includes 16 genes ($j = 1, 2 \ldots, 16$). Additionally, W_i indicates the weight of each attribute within service brand personality, that is, the ratio of the selected numbers for each attribute among respondents. People can select five of the 18 attributes. Similarly, W_j is the weight of genes among the service experience variable, that is, the rate at which customers selected "1." Once "0" appears in the set of service experience, we give ".5" as the penalty, which means that the service firm cannot exceed customer expectations and will result in customer dissatisfaction. Finally, this study sets $X_i = 9$ and $Y_j = 8$ as the constraints to avoid local optimization.

$$\text{Maximum } Z = (\textstyle\sum_{i=1}^{18} X_i W_j) \times [\textstyle\sum_{j=1}^{16} Y_j W_j - 0.5(16 - \textstyle\sum_{j=1}^{16} Y_j)],$$

s.t.

$X_i = 1$ (if the attribute i of service brand personality is selected); 0 (else),

$Y_j = 1$ (if the attribute j of service experience is selected); 0 (else),

$$W_i = \frac{\text{the selected numbers of each attribute of service brand personality}}{\text{the number of respondents} \times 5},$$

$$W_j = \frac{\text{the selected numbers of each attribute of service experience}}{\text{the number of respondents}},$$

Max X_i = 9; Max Y_j = 8

Two Restaurant Cases in Taiwan

For the selection of target service firms, we chose two steakhouses in Taiwan, owned by the Wang Group, as the observation objects. One is called "Wang Steak," and the other is called "TASTY." Although the Wang Group manages both steakhouses, these two steakhouses concentrate on different market segments and provide different service experiences. We collected 180 valid samples of TASTY. The obtained 180 samples consist of 61.7% female customers and 38.3% male customers. We classify customers into five apparel styles. The analysis result shows that the top two clothing styles are casual and elegant styles, which occupy 62.8% and 25.6%, respectively. Of the remaining 11.6% of customers, 10% wear modern styles, 1.1% wear sporty styles, and 0.6% wear formal styles. The obtained 95 samples of Wang Steak were derived from 60% female and 40% male customers. The analysis results show that the top two clothing styles are casual and elegant styles, which are 50.5% and 38.9%, respectively. Of the remaining 10.6% of customers, 9.5% wear fashionable styles and 1.1% wear formal styles.

Five Styles on TASTY and Wang Service Brand

Customers in the five apparel styles associate the TASTY service brand with sincerity (44%) more than competence (33%), excitement (11%), or sophistication (11%), and they score core service (37.5%) and employee service (37.5%) higher than servicescape (25%). People also regard TASTY as an "honest, sincere, wholesome, friendly, reliable, corporate, successful, unique, and glamorous" brand. Customers believe that the core service at TASTY is reliable and good, and it suits their needs. They have a good impression of neat employees and think that the facility suits the service type when mentioning servicescape. For employee service, customers believe that the service providers are courteous and willing to help them, which earns their trust.

In Figure 7.3, customers of Wang Steak associate the Wang service brand with competence (44%) more than sincerity (22%), sophistication (22%), or excitement (11%), and they score core service (60.5%) higher

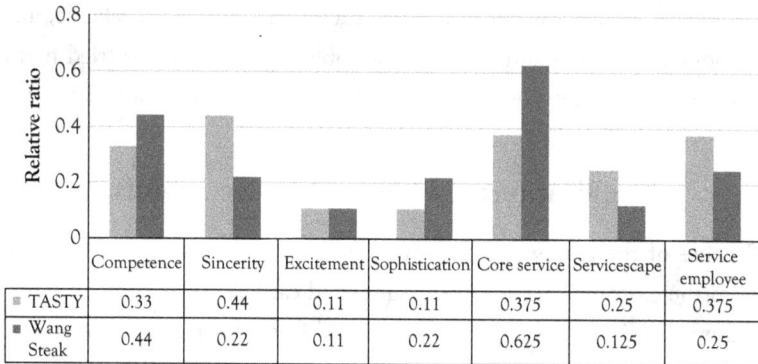

	Competence	Sincerity	Excitement	Sophistication	Core service	Servicescape	Service employee
▨ TASTY	0.33	0.44	0.11	0.11	0.375	0.25	0.375
▪ Wang Steak	0.44	0.22	0.11	0.22	0.625	0.125	0.25

Figure 7.3 Cross analysis on TASTY and Wang service brands

than employee service (25%) and servicescape (12.5%). Customers perceive "reliable, corporate, successful, confident, sincere, friendly, unique, upper-class, and glamorous" traits when thinking of the Wang service brand and consider the core service as superior in quality. Well-dressed and polite employees play a key role in the customer experience, and employees always show a willing attitude to help at Wang Steak.

The optimal service brands seem to be consistent with the brand spirits of TASTY and Wang Steak from the customer perspective. TASTY, a middle-end steakhouse, particularly provides vigorous, warm, and friendly service to customers. The analysis of the optimal service brand shows that customers perceive traits of sincerity including "honest, sincere, wholesome, and friendly" more than traits of competence, excitement, and sophistication. They score employee service and core service higher than servicescape. Wang Steak is a high-end steakhouse in the market segment and provides high-class services to customers. The study results show that customers associate the traits of "success, confidence, upper-class, glamour," and so forth with Wang Steak service. Customers also score core service higher than employee service and servicescape. This research refers to successful core services that indicate that only the best parts of ribs can be served to customers and the congruence between customer expectations and perception of provided services.

In summary, customers regard TASTY as an "honest, sincere, wholesome, and friendly" service brand, similar to a child who is picky about food (core service) and needs someone's attention and protection (employee service). Wang Steak is a "successful, confident, reliable, and corporate" service brand, similar to a noble woman who has tried many delicious dishes globally and is particular about taste (core service).

Implications for Mining Service Brands

Because of the emerging service-centered era, we explore service brand from the customer perspective. As indicted earlier, the existing literature is dominant in designing the service brand from the marketer viewpoint. However, our empirical findings indicate that if firms consider an optimal service brand from the customer perspective, they can evaluate whether the service brands customers perceive are consistent with the brands the firm attempts to build and deliver, similar to the case of the Wang Group. Firms can examine if the perceived differences between the service brands of two restaurants fit the market segment. Furthermore, our result shows that clothing can be a cue to show the customer image of a service brand. Realizing service brand optimization in the minds of customers with different apparel styles can help firms design various service experiences to satisfy customers who intentionally seek a specific service experience. Firms can manage customer expectations and perceptions more readily using tangible apparel cues to predict the abstract service image of customers. Clothing can influence customer perceptions of a service brand image because clothing can be a nonverbal form of communication. Firms can deliver a service brand image to customers by designing activities with a dress code requirement. Customers who wear appropriate clothing to a restaurant may perceive service brand personality and enjoy the service experience more easily.

In addition, realizing what the optimization of service brand is in the minds of customers can help firms create a unique service image, which can help them differentiate from competitors and gain a competitive edge in the service market. A firm can control key factors for a service image after understanding the key factors that affect customer imagination for service and the key elements that create customer value.[15] Firms can help themselves by sketching a service image and then planning better service delivery that is consistent with customer expectations and imagery of the service brand. For example, firms can enhance the overall customer service experience by designing external and internal experiences such as attractive advertisements, atmosphere, and shop décor to distribute production and facility investment efficiently and effectively and to improve aspects to create a high customer value.

In this chapter, the concept of service mining provides a novel viewpoint to look at service brands. Traditionally, the message of a service brand is determined and delivered by company. Service mining can help companies identify the service brand from customer viewpoint by their clothes. People usually dress more formal when they perceive the service environment is formal. Thus, customers can determine what service brands look like in a new mindset. Once the perceived service brand image is clear, the services will be improved and profit will be increased accordingly.

CHAPTER 8

Toward Service Idealism

This chapter discusses how the customer perceives the characteristics of an ideal service. The method used to analyze this aspect is genetic algorithm. This chapter covers the method (technology), scope (ideal service management), and domain (service in the restaurant) in as given in Figure 1.3. In this chapter, service mining is used to assist enterprises better understand what are the features of ideal services and modify the services accordingly.

The service sector has experienced significant growth in recent years. It has grown rapidly since 1970 and contributes handsomely to GDP in many countries worldwide. In some businesses, such as travel, tourism, catering, insurance, and banking businesses, the delivery of high-quality services to consumers is increasingly recognized as a key factor affecting the firm's performance.[1] Most companies use services to attract customers and gain their trust.

Recent research on services has shown that personal values may play a significant role in how consumers evaluate the quality of services and how it relates to their relationship with the firm.[2] Service providers can increase consumer intentions by providing ideal services. Customers feel satisfied with the services rendered by service providers. Therefore, with the intention of attracting more customers, service providers must provide ideal services expected by customers, described as service idealism. Services are unlike goods because they are intangible and cannot be touched, seen, or physically transported.

The concept of service idealism plays an important role in current discussions of the service sector. Despite widespread use of the term, there is still much to learn on what exactly service idealism is, what function it plays, and how managers can best address their authority. Service idealism focuses on what consumers need, and the admirable aspects of services in their minds. Service idealism strives for positive consequences, the right perception, and idealistic customer expectations of the service. Service idealism has a significant effect on decision making. Service idealism can also serve as a tool for understanding the optimal expectations of customers. Highly idealistic consumers believe that the optimal service of the service provider has positive consequences and meets traditional consumer expectations. Idealistic people generally believe that the right behavior always leads to positive consequences.

To perceive the service idealism of the customer, the service provider must know the customer's characteristics. Hence, a service provider must understand the personality traits of the customer. Personality traits are influenced by the distinctive and the implicit, personal knowledge, values/beliefs, perceptions, and experiences of an individual, and cannot be simulated easily.[3] In this chapter, we use human psychology to determine the relationship between the components of service idealism and customer personality. We also discover components that affect service idealism for the service provider. Finally, the genetic algorithm (GA) was used to find the optimal result of service idealism based on customer perception and personality.

Service Idealism Framework

Service idealism can be defined as the services of the provider perceived to be in accordance with customer expectations. We assume that the factor that affects the view of a customer is the most important element of service idealism. To identify service idealism as it relates to the customer, it is necessary to find the optimal component of service idealism based on customer personality. At a basic level, we use the personality traits of the customer to identify the components that have an impact on service idealism. Personality plays an important role in individual and organizational relationships.[4] The big five model of personality provides a widely recognized taxonomy of personality dimensions and has been accepted as a higher order factor that helps characterize and better understand other personality constructs.[5] The big five personality framework (extraversion, agreeableness, conscientiousness, neuroticism, and openness) has received considerable support in psychology over the past 20 years.

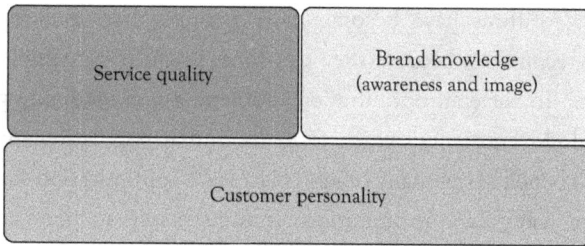

Figure 8.1 *Service idealism model*

Therefore, two components are identified to optimize service idealism (Figure 8.1). First, service quality is the capability of a provider to shape the character of a primarily intangible service to meet specific standards based on customer expectations. Most of the researchers found that customer satisfaction is influenced by service quality.[6] Second, brand knowledge is one of the most important concepts related to marketing science. Because brand knowledge can strongly influence customer purchasing behavior, it can be concluded that brand knowledge is an important component that simultaneously reflects the ideas of consumers regarding the product and service. Numerous researchers have shown that brand knowledge consists of two dimensions: brand awareness and brand image.[7] Brand image creates purchasing motivations of emotion, self-expressiveness, social, and connection aspects. Brand awareness is determined by how closely the image of the service provider matches the expectations of the consumer. Brand knowledge (brand awareness and image) affects consumer response to the brand. Brand knowledge has a direct relationship with customer preference.[8]

Optimizing Ideal Services

Genetic algorithms (GAs) are adaptive experimental exploration algorithms based on the evolutionary concepts of natural selection and genetics and are a part of evolutionary computing. Although GAs are randomized, they use historical information to direct the search toward better performance within the search space. In nature, competition among organisms over limited resources results in the fittest dominating over the weak.

Genetic algorithms have become more popular than traditional optimization techniques because they can solve irregular or complex fitness functions.[9] To solve an optimization problem, a GA randomly generates individual chromosomes, which form the initial population. A GA has important benefits over many other typical search optimization techniques.

Before using GA optimization, it is necessary to perform binary encoding. The GA starts from a seed population that generates (N) individuals. Table 8.1 shows the components of service idealism for gene size and bit orders in the chromosome. The layout of each chromosome is then used to discover the optimal chromosome for service idealism; that is, bits 1 to 16 for service quality and bits 17 to 24 for brand knowledge.

In particular, the fitness function of the strings can be calculated using Eq. (8.1). The objective function (f) is defined the optimal result relationship between two components of service idealism with customer personality:

$$\text{Fitness function } (f) = \text{MaxA} + \text{MaxB} \qquad (8.1)$$

where A is the service quality and B the brand knowledge. This study uses optimal results for setting the fitness function. The fitness function discovers the optimal result of service idealism observed from perceptions of customer personality. This conceptual framework uses two parts (MaxA + MaxB) to represent the sum of maximum values for A and B The best result toward service idealism is influenced by service quality and brand knowledge. We also use constraints in the proposed fitness

Table 8.1 Factors and components of service idealism

Factors		Attributes	Gene size (bits)	Bit orders in chromosome
Service quality	SQ	Reliability	16	1–4
		Responsiveness		5–7
		Assurance		8–10
		Empathy		11–13
		Tangible		14–16
Brand knowledge	BK	Awareness	8	17–20
		Image		21–24

function. To prevent the convergence of the maximum value in each component, it is necessary to include constraints in the fitness function.

$$\text{Subject to: Max}A = \sum_{i=1}^{16} X_i \times W_i, \qquad X_i = 1 \text{ or } 0$$

$$\text{Max}B = \sum_{i=1}^{8} X_i \times W_i, \qquad X_i = 1 \text{ or } 0$$

$$\textit{Constraint: } A \sum_{i=1}^{16} X_i = 8, X_i = 1 \text{ or } 0 \text{ service quality}$$

$$B \sum_{i=1}^{8} X_i = 4, X_i = 1 \text{ or } 0 \text{ brand knowledge}$$

The weight of each item (W_i) can be obtained from the size of each element ($X = 1$) divided by the number of items (N). Using constraints for each component helps avoid redundancy of each item. The constraints of service quality and brand knowledge were set as Constraint A and Constraint B. In this concept, restricted service quality ($X_i = 8$) and brand knowledge ($X_i = 4$) indicate that a Constraint A value of less than or more than 8 and Constraint B values of less than or more than 4 do not affect the order of each element in the chromosome.

Real Cases of Restaurants in Taiwan

This study uses two restaurants (TASTY and Wang Steak) that are part of the Wowprime Group in its analysis. These two restaurants are well-known steak restaurants in Taiwan and offer superior services. The priority of both restaurants is to provide good services to the customer, and both restaurants are primarily steak restaurants. The major differences between the two restaurants are that Wang Steak has a high-price menu, whereas TASTY offers a mid-price menu. We asked customers to fill out the questionnaire how they perceive service quality and brand of two restaurants. In addition, customers need to provide a self-report on their personalities in order to match customer personality and perception of service. The number of questionnaires collected from both restaurants was 418, and 402 questionnaires were valid. The number of respondents for TASTY was 290, whereas Wang Steak had 112. The population for the GA was 402 and represents respondents who had dined at either of the steak restaurants.

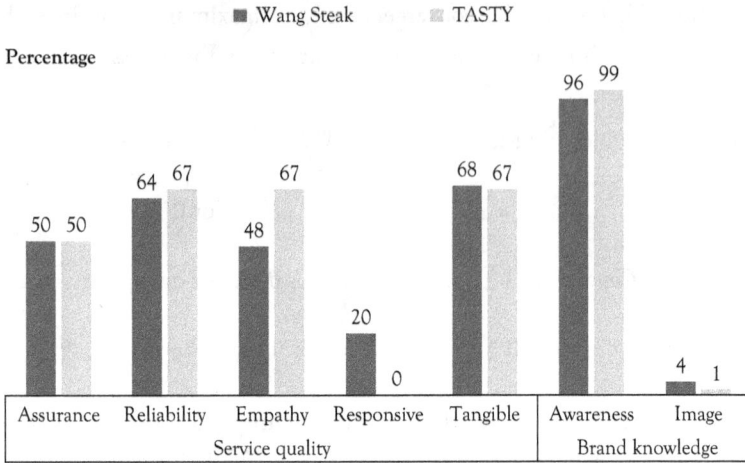

Figure 8.2 Service idealism between Wang Steak and TASTY

Figure 8.2 shows the optimal combination for the two restaurants based on GA analysis. The results show that customer personality is associated with customer expectations of service idealism. This result shows that customer expectations of service idealism for the two restaurants are significantly different. Customers who dine at TASTY expect are more reliability and empathy. Customers who dine at Wang Steak expect more responsiveness and brand image. Customers who dine at both restaurants are more affected in terms of awareness from the restaurant. TASTY and Wang Steak are famous steak restaurants in Taiwan. Both restaurants provide comfortable facilities and a benign atmosphere. Thus, there is no significant difference in tangibility and brand knowledge traits between the two restaurants. Overall, service idealism is positively affected by service quality and brand knowledge.

Based on these results, service quality and brand awareness both affect service idealism. Figure 8.2 also shows that service quality and brand knowledge have a significant effect on service idealism. The responsiveness of service restaurants and brand image do not have a significant effect on service idealism. From the viewpoint of brand image and responsiveness, customers probably have the image of the restaurant in mind in advance. Thus, prompt services may not significantly affect customer perceptions. Awareness of the restaurant plays a more important role than other items.

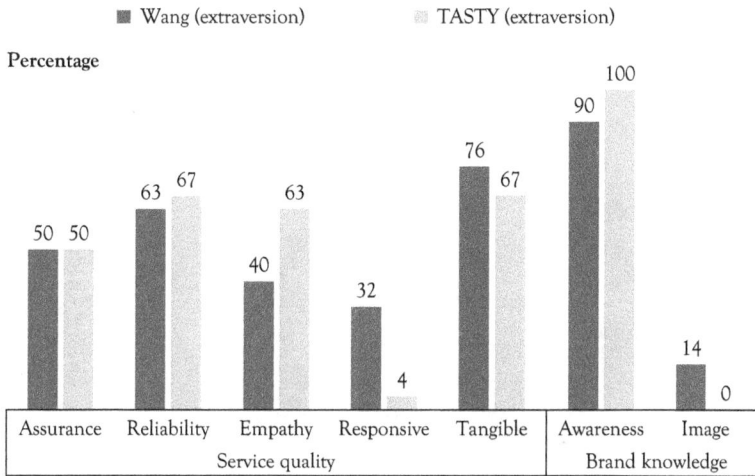

Figure 8.3 Service idealism by extraversion personality

This result shows that both restaurants have a good reputation in the industry, have well-established brand names, and enjoy good word-of-mouth recommendations. The results show that customer personalities positively affect customer perceptions of service idealism.

Customers who have an extrovert personality exhibit more sociability, activity, assertiveness, and positive emotionality characteristics. Based on extraversion personality, reliability, empathy, and assurance have a significant effect on customer perceptions of service quality in the two restaurants (Figure 8.3). Customers who dine at TASTY are more influenced by empathy and reliability in service quality. Customer who dine at Wang Steak are more influenced by responsiveness and tangible service quality. Brand knowledge shows a significant difference between Wang Steak and TASTY restaurants. Extrovert customers are more influenced by brand awareness. Figure 8.3 shows that customers who dine at TASTY are totally influenced by brand awareness. Brand image has no effect on customers with an extraversion personality with regard to the TASTY restaurant. Customers with extraversion personality are more influenced by brand image when they dine at the Wang Steak restaurant. This result makes it clear that customers with extraversion personality will expect more brand image and responsive service when they dine in a high-end restaurant.

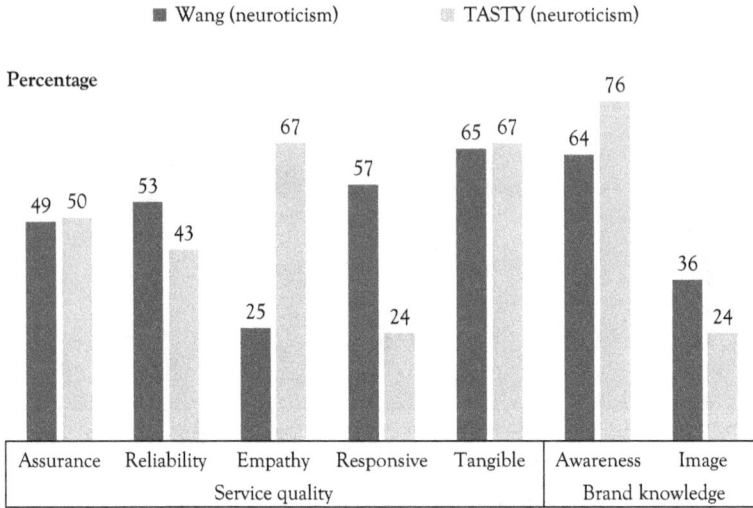

■ Wang (neuroticism)   ▨ TASTY (neuroticism)

Percentage

Figure 8.4 Service idealism by neuroticism personality

Customers with neuroticism personality display negative emotions such as feeling anxious, nervous, sad, irritable, drowsy, and tense. Overall, service tangibility and brand awareness are the most important elements that affect customers with partial neuroticism personality toward service idealism. Figure 8.4 shows the differences between two restaurants in terms of customers with a neurotic personality. Customer perception of service assurance and tangibility of the two restaurants have no significant differences. This result shows that customers who have a neurotic personality have the same standard of assurance and service tangibility from both the restaurants. Customers with a neurotic personality generally have negative emotions and uncertainty in mood or feeling. The significant differences of personality between two restaurants are empathy and responsiveness. Customers dining at TASTY are more influenced by service empathy. Customers expect individual attention and employees should understand this need of the customers. However, customers dining at Wang Steak are influenced more by responsiveness of service quality. Customers expect more prompt services and readiness to respond to customers' requests.

Agreeableness refers to traits such as altruism, tender-heartedness, trust, gentleness, love, reliability, and modesty. Customers who have

■ Wang (agreeableness)   ▨ TASTY (agreeableness)

Percentage

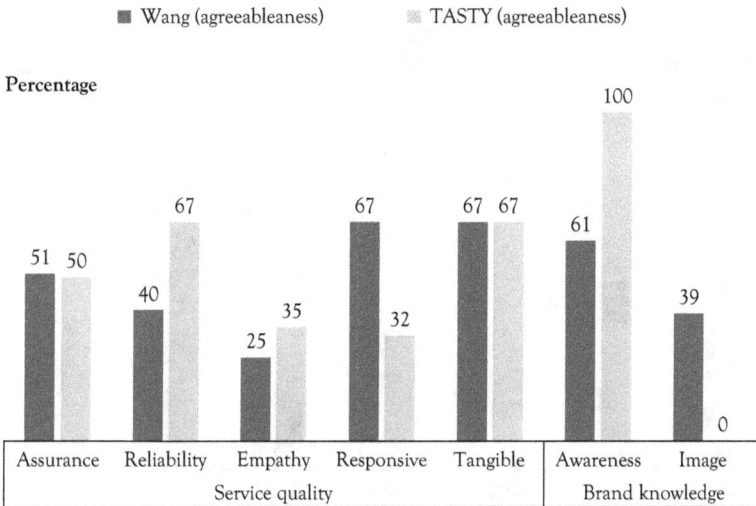

Figure 8.5 Service idealism by agreeableness personality

an agreeable personality are more influenced by service responsiveness of Wang Steak restaurant and service reliability of TASTY restaurant (Figure 8.5). Customer perception of service tangibility and assurance from two restaurants has no significant difference. Customers who dine at TASTY are influenced more by service reliability. Customers expect services to be provided at the right time and right place. Brand awareness is the most important element for customers who dine at TASTY. Customers who display an agreeable personality in TASTY restaurant are more influenced by awareness of the restaurant. Customers who dine at Wang Steak are more influenced by service responsiveness. This result shows that customers will expect more information and the readiness to respond to customers' request from Wang Steak restaurant. Brand image also plays an important role in affecting customer perceptions.

Conscientiousness describes the task and goal-directed behavior of highly motivated, ambitious, and detail-oriented people. Customers who have a conscientiousness personality have significant differences on expectation toward service idealism of the two restaurants. Customers who dine in the two restaurants have different perceptions of service. Brand awareness is the most important element to affect customers at TASTY, while service tangibility is the most important element to affect customers who have a conscientiousness personality and dine at Wang Steak.

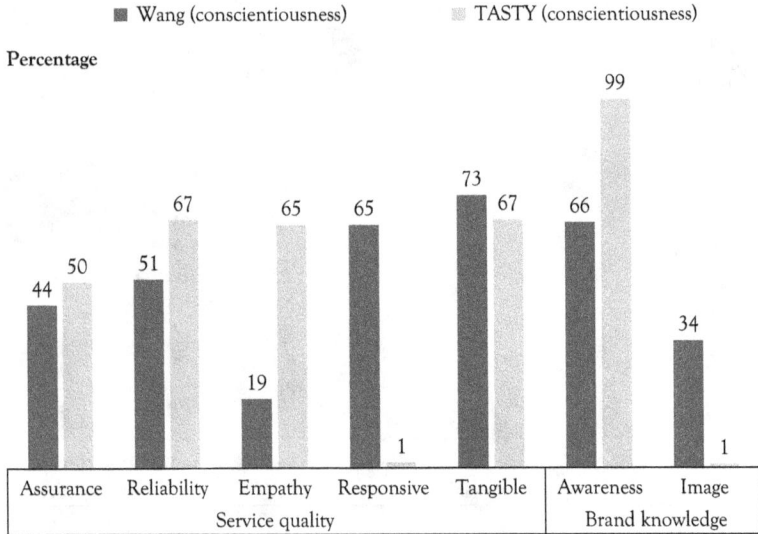

Figure 8.6 *Service idealism by conscientiousness personality*

Responsive service and brand image have no significant effect on customers in TASTY. Furthermore, brand image and service responsiveness are important elements of service idealism in Wang Steak (Figure 8.6). This result reveals that the higher price we pay, we expect more responsiveness and brand image from the restaurant.

Figure 8.7 shows that customer perception toward service idealism based on openness personality of the customers for the two restaurants. Imagination, different interests, creativity, and originality are some openness traits. Customers who have a open personality are more imaginative in thinking than the others. Service tangibility and assurance of two restaurants have no significant differences. Customers who are open have the same perception about service tangibility and assurance of two restaurants. Service responsiveness and brand image have no significant effect on customers at TASTY but responsiveness is an important factor affecting customers at Wang Steak.

Look Toward the Future

The results provide evidence for ideal service optimization. Firstly, the results show that each component of service idealism plays an important

■ Wang (openness)   ■ TASTY (openness)

Percentage

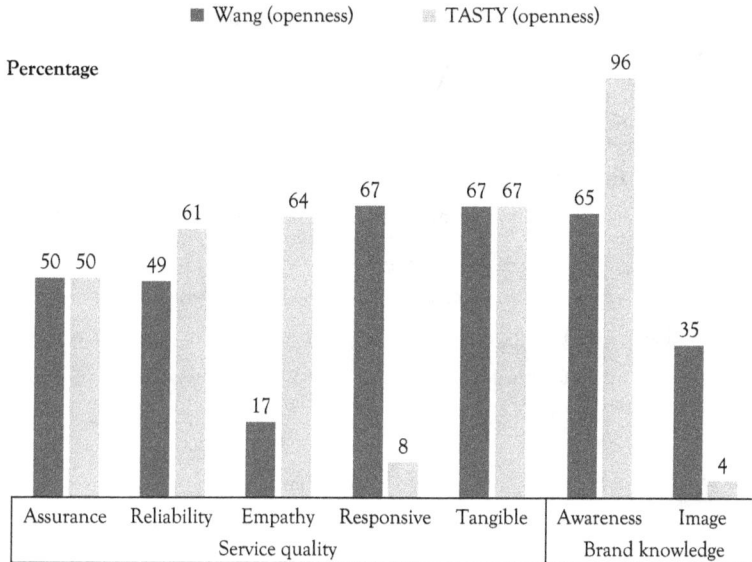

Figure 8.7 Service idealism by openness personality

role on customer perceptions of service. Service idealism for both restaurants is significantly influenced by "brand awareness" and "tangible
service." Secondly, results show that customer personality traits influence
customer perceptions of services by confirming the theory of personality psychology. Customers who exhibit an extrovert personality are more
influenced by reliability and awareness of restaurant, while customers
with a neurotic personality are more influenced by empathy and brand
image. Customers with an agreeable personality are more influenced by
responsiveness, conscientiousness, while those with an open personality
are more influenced by brand awareness and service tangibility.

In other words, the concept of service idealism may contribute to
existing service sectors. First, the components affecting customer perception can help companies improve their services. Service providers in
different domains can examine customer perceptions of service idealism.
Second, customer personality traits are important factors for classifying
customers. Firms can increase customer loyalty and impressions by adopt-
ing the concept of service idealism based on personality traits. In other
words, understanding customer personality traits is the best approach to
succeed in the service industry. Finally, the results provide clues for other

restaurants (i.e., not only steak restaurants) to furnish superior services to attract customers.

In this chapter, the concept of service mining provides a novel viewpoint to look at what an ideal service might be from the customer viewpoint. Typically, an ideal service must satisfy customer demands. The theory of big five personality can assist enterprises examine each service in different dimensions. Thus, the shape of an ideal service can be optimized from customer responses. Service mining eventually will help firms identify good services and ideal services to customers. This also may result in better profit and benefit compared to the existing mindset.

Conclusion

This book proposes a novel research area, service mining, which differs from the notion of service science and provides a comprehensive and holistic framework. Service mining comprises of five elements: Infrastructure, technology, modeling, management, and application. The service lifecycle of service mining includes service discovery, experience, recovery, and retention. Excepting the phase of design in service lifecycle, each chapter synthesizes the concepts of four phases, including discovery (Chapters 2, 5, and 8), experience (Chapters 3, 4, 6, and 8), recovery (Chapter 6), and retention/loyalty (Chapter 5). This book also addresses the emergent issues among five elements that combine technology and management perspectives. Compared to web service and service science, service mining completely combines computer science and social science as a new mindset. Service mining goes beyond the existing service management and is considered as a branch of service science. Service mining is also different from data mining in the service domain. The concept of data mining focuses on collected data from value cocreation. However, the concept of service mining not only investigates data from interactions but also focuses on the features of services. This book provides several issues in services, including customer value (Chapter 2), service pricing (Chapter 3), service cooperation (Chapter 4), prediction of service in customer relationship management (Chapter 5), service failure and recovery (Chapter 6), service branding (Chapter 7), and service idealism (Chapter 8). Each chapter not only introduces the concept but also provides the real-world applications to illustrate the idea. Algorithm of computer science, modeling from operations research, and simulation from system dynamics are used to help readers better understand the linkage between concept and practice. Meanwhile, management is also embedded in each issue. After reading this book, the readers would be able to understand what service mining is and how to apply and extend the concept to new service problems, for example, service alliance. Service mining is not the perspective of computer science but also the perspective of multiple disciplines to look into services. Enterprises can reexamine the service lifecycle to discover the problems. Adjustment and revision may be needed to modify the entire service process. Service mining can provide a different viewpoint for firms to reconsider the appropriate actions for service. The discussed topics also can give companies a new mindset to look into service issues. More issues can be investigated and discussed in the future, for example, strategic alliance in services from the service provider perspective, modeling service experience from the customer perspective, the components of service atmosphere that affect customer perception from both sides, or any other e-services issues. Practitioners can link problems occurring in services from real world and the concepts in this book to stimulate ideas for solutions. This book aims to build a new stream of service with a novel concept and identify the potential opportunities for academia and practice.

Notes

Chapter 1

1. Rust and Miu (2006).
2. Bolton (2003).
3. Hoffman (2003).
4. Maglio and Spohrer (2008).
5. Song (2003).
6. Savoy and Dolamic (2009).
7. Bitner, Ostrom, and Morgan (2008).
8. Tung and Yuan (2010); Chang, Yuan, and Li (2009).
9. Song, Song, and Benedtto (2009); Rust and Chung (2006); Roels, Karmarkar, and Carr (2010).
10. Jong and Ruyter (2004); Schmenner (2004); Ghose, Mukhopadhyay, and Rajan (2007); Chellappa and Kumar (2005); Chang, Yuan, and Li (2010); Galup, Dattero, Quan, and Conger (2009).
11. Song (2003); Heim, Wentworth, and Peng (2009).

Chapter 2

1. Liu, Sudharshan, and Hamer (2000).
2. Tung and Yuan (2008).
3. Berger and Nada (1998).
4. Scupola (2008).
5. Dwyer (1989); Mulhern (1999).
6. Parasuraman, Zeithaml, and Berry (1988); Cronin and Taylor (1992); Brown, Churchill, and Peter (1993).
7. Dwyer (1989); Nadeem (2006); Mulhern (1999).
8. Nadeem (2006).
9. Dwyer (1989); Nadeem (2006).

Chapter 3

1. Leung and Fung (1996); Al-Fedaghi and Al-Behairy (2011).
2. Rust and Kannan (2003).
3. Zeithaml, Parasuraman, and Malhotra (2000); Zeithaml, Parasuraman, and Malhotra (2002); Wolfinbarger and Gilly (2003).

4. Leung and Fung (1996).
5. Ren, Liu, and Lv (2011).
6. Zeithaml (1988).

Chapter 4

1. Rowley (2006); Venkatesan, Chellappan, and Dhavachelvan (2010).
2. Liu, Shen, and Liao (2003).
3. Tiwana and Ramesh (2001).
4. Marciukaityte, Roskelley, and Wang (2009); ul-Haq and Howcroft (2006); Ku and Fan (2009); Strate and Rappole (1997).
5. Allee (2000).
6. Brouther and Keith (1995).
7. Michael, Edward, Edhec, and Borze (2000).
8. Li and Rowley (2002).
9. Allee (2000).
10. Clarke and Flaherty (2003).
11. Chiou and Shen (2006).
12. McAlpine and Myles (2003).
13. Crnec and Seljan (2010).
14. Chen and Hsieh (2000).

Chapter 5

1. Gupta, Lehmann, and Stuart (2004).
2. Kolter (1997).
3. Edvardsson, Enquist, and Johnston (2005).
4. Ling and Yen (2001).
5. Albrecht (1992).

Chapter 6

1. Skaaning (2005).
2. Reichheld and Sasser (1990).
3. Rousseau, Sitkin, Burt, and Camerer (1998).
4. Reichheld and Schefter (2000).
5. Ribbink, Riel, Liljander, and Streukens (2004); Gefen and Straub (2004); Kim, Zhao, and Yang (2008); Kim, Jin, and Swinney (2009); Chiu, Huang, and Yen (2010).
6. Wu (2011).

7. Kotler (1997).
8. Liao and Wu (2009).
9. Miller, Craighead, and Karwan (2000); Maxham (2001); Sousa and Voss (2009).
10. Holloway and Beatty (2003).
11. Sterman (2000).
12. Miller, Craighead, and Karwan (2000).

Chapter 7

1. Hume (2008); Brodie, Glynn, and Little (2006).
2. Ogba and Tan (2009).
3. Chang, Hsu, and Chaung (2008).
4. Malik and Naeem (2011); Wu, Yeh, and Hsiao (2011); Hosany, Ekinci, and Uysal (2007); Padgett and Allen (1997); Shen and Liao (2007).
5. Kaiser (1983).
6. Shao, Baker, and Wagner (2004).
7. Aziz, Ghani, and Niazi (2010); Padgett and Allen (1997).
8. Aaker (1997).
9. Musante, Bojanic, and Zhang (2008).
10. Grace and O'Cass (2004).
11. Orsingher and Marzocchi (2003).
12. Kaiser (1983).
13. Kwon (1988).
14. Ulrich, Anderson-Connell, and Wu (2003); Lin (2007).
15. Zomerdijk and Voss (2010).

Chapter 8

1. Atilgan, Akinici, and Aksoy (2003).
2. Lages and Fernandes (2005).
3. Kor, Mahonay, and Michael (2007).
4. Güney (2008).
5. John and Srivastava (1999).
6. Bedi (2010); Kassim and Abdullah (2010); Kumar, Mani, Mahalingam, and Vanjikovan (2010).
7. Aaker (1996); Huang (2011).
8. Keller (2003).
9. Changyu, Lixia, and Qian (2007); Fang, Ni, and Yu (2009).

References

Aaker, D. A. (1996). Measuring brand equity across products and markets. *California Management Review 38*(3), 102–120.

Aaker, J. L. (1997). Dimensions of brand personality. *Journal of Marketing Research 34*(3), 347–356.

Albrecht, K. (1992). *The only thing that matters: Bringing the customer to the center of your business.* New York, NY: Harper Business.

Al-Fedaghi, S. S., & Al-Behairy, S. A. (2011). Personal identifiable information and laws: The case of financial services. *AISS: Advances in Information Sciences and Service Sciences 3*(5), 126–138.

Allee, V. (2000). Reconfiguring the value network. *Journal of Business Strategy 21*(4), 36–39. doi:10.1108/eb040103

Atilgan, E., Akinici, S., & Aksoy, S. (2003). Mapping service quality in tourism industry. *Managing Service Quality 13*, 412–422.

Aziz, S., Ghani, U., & Niazi, M. A. K. (2010). Measuring brand personalities of cellular service providers of Pakistan. *Institute of Interdisciplinary Business Research 2*(6), 473–483.

Bedi, M. (2010). An integrated framework for service quality, customer satisfaction and behavioural responses in Indian Banking industry: A comparison of public and private sector banks. *Journal of Services Research 10*(1), 157–172.

Berger, P. D., & Nada, I. N. (1998). Customer lifetime value: Marketing models and applications. *Journal of Interactive Marketing 12*(1), 17–30.

Bitner, M. J., Ostrom, A. L., & Morgan, F. N. (2008). Service blueprinting: A practical technique for service innovation. *California Management Review 50*(3), 66–94.

Bolton, R. N. (2003). Marketing challenges of e-services. *Communications of the ACM 46*(6), 43–44.

Brodie, R. J., Glynn, M. S., & Little, V. (2006). The service brand and the service-dominant logic: Missing fundamental premise or the need for stronger theory. *Marketing Theory 6*(3), 363–379.

Brouther, W., & Keith, D. (1995). Strategic alliances: Choose your partners. *Journal of Long Rang Planning 28*(3), 18–25. doi:10.1016/0024-6301(95)00008-7

Brown, T. J., Churchill Jr., G. A., & Peter, J. P. (1993). Improving the measurement of service quality. *Journal of Retailing 69*(1), 127–139.

Chang, H. H., Hsu, C.-H., & Chaung, S. H. (2008). The antecedents and consequences of brand equity in service markets. *Asia Pacific Management Review 13*(3), 601–624.

Chang, W. L., Yuan, S. T., & Hsu, C. W. (2010). Creating the experience economy in e-commerce. *Communications of the ACM 53*(7), 122–127.

Chang, W. L., Yuan, S. T., & Li, E. Y. (2009). iCare home portal: An extended model of quality aging e-services. *Communications of the ACM 52*(11), 118–124.

Changyu, S., Lixia, W., & Qian, L. (2007). Optimization of injection molding process parameters using combination of artificial neural network and genetic algorithm method. *Journal Mater Process Technology 183*, 412–418.

Chellappa, R. K., & Kumar, K. R. (2005). Examining the role of "Free" product-augmenting online services in pricing and customer retention strategies. *Journal of Management Information Systems 22*(1), 355–377.

Chen, S. H., & Hsieh, C. H. (2000). Representation, ranking, distance, and similarity of L-R type fuzzy number and application. *Australian Journal of Intelligent Processing System 6*, 217–229.

Chiou, J. S., & Shen, C. C. (2006). The effects of satisfaction, opportunism, and asset specificity on customers' loyalty intention toward Internet portal sites. *Journal of Service Industry Management 17*(1), 7–22. doi:10.1108/09564230610651552

Chiu, C. M., Huang, H. Y., & Yen, C. H. (2010). Antecedents of trust in online auctions. *Electronic Commerce Research and Applications 9*, 148–159.

Clarke, I., & Flaherty, T. B. (2003). Web-based B2B portals. *Journal of Industrial Marketing Management 32*(1), 15–23. doi:10.1016/S0019-8501(01)00199-7

Crnec, D., & Seljan, S. (2010, May). *Evaluation of open-source online dictionaries.* MIPRO, Opatija, Croatia, Proceeding of the 33rd International Convention, pp. 858–862.

Cronin, J. J., & Taylor, S. A. (1992). Measuring service quality: A re-examination and extension. *Journal of Marketing 56*, 55–68.

Dwyer, F. R. (1989). Customer lifetime profitability to support marketing decision making. *Journal of Direct Marketing 3*(4), 8–15.

Edvardsson, B., Enquist, B., & Johnston, R. (2005). Cocreating customer value through hyperreality in the prepurchase service experience. *Journal of Service Research 8*(2), 149–161.

Fang, F., Ni, B., & Yu, H. (2009). Estimating the kinetic parameters of activated sludge storage using weighted non-linear least-squares and accelerating genetic algorithm. *Water Res 43*, 2595–2604.

Galup, S. D., Dattero, D., Quan, J. J., & Conger, S. (2009). An overview of IT service management. *Communications of the ACM 52*(5), 124–127.

Gefen, D., & Straub, D. W. (2004). Consumer trust in B2C e-Commerce and the importance of social presence: Experiments in e-Products and e-Services. *The International Journal of Management Science 32*, 407–424.

Ghose, A., Mukhopadhyay, T., & Rajan, U. (2007). The impact of Internet referral services on a supply chain. *Information Systems Research 18*(3), 300–319.

Grace, D., & O'Cass, A. (2004). Examing service experiences and post-consumption evaluations. *The Journal of Services Marketing 18*(6), 450–461.

Güney, S. (2008). *Davranış Bilimleri* (4th ed.). Ankara: Nobel.

Gupta, S., Lehmann, D., & Stuart, J. (2004). Valuing customer. *Journal of Marketing Research 41*(1), 7–18.

Heim, G. R., Wentworth Jr., W. R., & Peng, X. (2009). The value to the customer of RFID in service applications. *Decision Sciences 40*(3), 477–512.

Hoffman, K. D. (2003). Marketing + mis = e-service. *Communications of the ACM 46*(6), 53–55.

Holloway, B. B., & Beatty, S. E. (2003). Service failure in online retailing, a recovery opportunity. *Journal of Service Research 6*(1), 92–103.

Hosany, S., Ekinci, Y., & Uysal, M. (2007). Destination image and destination personality. *International Journal of Culture, Tourism and Hospitality Research 1*(1), 62–81.

Huang, M. H. (2011). Re-examining the effect of service recovery: The moderating role of brand equity. *Journal of Service Marketing 25*(7), 509–516.

Hume, M. (2008). Developing a conceptual model for repurchase intention in the performing arts: The roles of emotions, core service and service delivery. *International Journal of Arts Management 10*(2), 40–55.

John, O. P., & Srivastava, S. (1999). The big five trait taxonomy: History, measurement, and theoretical perspectives. In L. A. Pervin & O. P. John (Eds.), *Handbook of personality: Theory and research* (2nd Ed.). New York, NY: Guilford.

Jong, A., & Ruyter, K. (2004). Adaptive versus proactive behavior in service recovery: The role of self-managing teams. *Decision Sciences 35*(3), 457–491.

Kaiser, S. B. (1983). Toward a contextual social psychology of clothing: a synthesis of symbolic interactionist and cognitive theoretical perspectives. *Clothing and Textiles Research Journal 2*, 1–9.

Kassim, N., & Abdullah, N. A. (2010). The effect of perceived service quality dimensions on customer satisfaction, trust, and loyalty in e-commerce settings: A cross cultural analysis. *Asia Pacific Journal of Marketing and Logistics 22*(3), 351–371.

Keller, K. L. (2003). *Strategic brand management, building, measuring, and managing brand equity* (2nd Ed.). Upper Saddle River, NJ: Prentice Hall.

Kim, C., Zhao, W., & Yang, K. H. (2008). An empirical study on the integrated framework of e-CRM in online shopping: Evaluating the relationships among perceived value, satisfaction, and trust based on customers' perspectives. *Journal of Electronic Commerce in Organizations 6*(3), 1–19.

Kim, J., Jin, B., & Swinney, J. L. (2009). The role of etail quality, e-satisfaction and e-trust in online loyalty development process. *Journal of Retailing and Consumer Services 16*, 239–247.

Kor, Y. Y., Mahoney, J. T., & Michael, S. C. (2007). Resources, capabilities and entrepreneurial perception. *Journal of Management Studies 44*(7), 1187–1212.

Kotler, P. (1997a). Marketing management, analysis, implementation and using the servoual model. *The Service Industries Journal 11*(3), 324–343.

Kotler, P. (1997b). *Marketing management: Analysis, planning, implementation, and control.* Upper Saddle River, NJ: Prentice Hall.

Ku, E. C. S., & Fan, Y. W. (2009). Knowledge sharing and customer relationship management in the travel service alliances. *Journal of Total Quality Management 20*(12), 1407–1421.

Kumar, S. A., Mani, B. T., Mahalingam, S., & Vanjikovan, M. (2010). Influence of service quality on attitudinal loyalty in private retail banking: An empirical study. *Journal of Management Research 9*(4), 21–38.

Kwon, Y.-H. (1988). Effects of situational and individual influences on the selection of daily clothing. *Clothing and Textiles Research Journal 6*(4), 6–12.

Lages, L. F., & Fernandes, J. C. (2005). The SERPVAL scale: A multi-item instrument for measuring service personal values. *Journal of Business Research 58*(11), 1562–1572.

Leung, C., & Fung, M. W. (1996). Assessing perceived service quality of casual-wear chain stores. *Journal of Fashion Marketing and Management 1*(1), 26–49.

Li, S. X., & Rowley, T. J. (2002). Inertia and evaluation mechanisms in interorganizational partner selection: Syndicate formation among US investment banks. *Journal of Academy of management 45*(6), 1104–1119.

Liao, N. N. H., & Wu, T. C. (2009). The pivotal role of trust in customer loyalty: Empirical research on the system integration market in Taiwan. *The Business Review 12*(2), 277–282.

Lin, J.-J. (2007). Intelligent decision making based on GA for creative apparel styling. *Journal of Information Science and Engineering 23*, 1923–1937.

Ling, R., & Yen, D. C. (2001). Customer relationship management: An analysis framework and implementation strategies. *Journal of Computer Information Systems 41*, 82–97.

Liu, B. S., Sudharshan, D., & Hamer, L. O. (2000). After-service response in service quality assessment: A real-time updating model approach. *Journal of Service Marketing 14*(2), 160–177.

Liu, D. R., Shen, M., & Liao, C. T. (2003). Designing a composite e-service platform with recommendation function. *Computer Standards & Interfaces 25*(2), 103–117.

Maglio, P. P., & Spohrer, J. (2008). Fundamentals of service science. *Journal of the Academic Marketing Science 36*, 18–20.

Malik, M. E., & Naeem, B. (2011). Interrelationship between customer based brand equity constructs: Empirical evidence from hotel industry of Pakistan. *Interdisciplinary Journal of Contemporary Research in Business 3*(4), 795–804.

Marciukaityte, D., Roskelley, K., & Wang, H. (2009). Strategic alliances by financial services firms. *Journal of Business Research 62*(11), 1193–1199. doi:10.1016/j.jbusres.2008.07.004

Maxham, J. G. (2001). Service recovery's influence on consumer satisfaction, positive word-of-mouth, and purchase intentions. *Journal of Business Research 54*, 11–24.

McAlpine, J., & Myles, J. (2003). Capturing phraseology in an online dictionary for advanced users of English as a second language: A response to user needs. *System 31*(1), 71–84.

Michael, A. H. M. T. D., Edward, L., Edhec, J. L. A., & Borze, A. (2000). Partner selection in emerging and developed market contexts: Resource-based and organizational learning perspectives. *Journal of Academy of Management 43*(3), 449–467.

Miller, J. L., Craighead, C. W., & Karwan, K. R. (2000). Service recovery: A framework and empirical investigation. *Journal of Operations Management 18*(4), 387–400.

Mulhern, F. J. (1999). Customer profitability analysis: Measurement, concentration, and research directions. *Journal of Interactive Marketing 13*(1), 25–40.

Musante, M. D., Bojanic, D. C., & Zhang, J. (2008). A modified brand personality scale for the restaurant industry. *Journal of Hospitality & Leisure Marketing 16*(4), 303–323.

Nadeem, M. (2006). How leadership results in return on customer, and customer lifetime value. *The Business Review, Cambridge 6*(1), 218–224.

Ogba, I.-E., & Tan, Z. (2009). Exploring the impact of brand image on customer loyalty and commitment in China. *Journal of Technology Management in China 4*(2), 132–144.

Orsingher, C., & Marzocchi, G. L. (2003). Hierarchical representation of satisfactory consumer service experience. *International Journal of Service Industry Management 14*(2), 200–216.

Padgett, D., & Allen, D. (1997). Communicating experiences: A narrative approach to creating service brand image. *Journal of Advertising 26*(4), 49–62.

Parasuraman, A., Zeithaml, V. A., & Berry, L. L. (1988). SERVQUAL: A multiple-item scale for measuring customer perceptions of service quality. *Journal of Retailing 64*(1), 12–40.

Reichheld, F. F., & Sasser, W. E. (1990, September–October). Zero defections: Quality comes to services. *Harvard Business Review* 105–111.

Reichheld, F. F., & Schefter, P. (2000). E-loyalty: Your secret weapon on the web. *Harvard Business Review 78*, 105–113.

Ren, X., Liu, L., & Lv, C. (2011). Ranking sellers in C2C sites: A hedonic price approach. *Journal of Convergence Information Technology 6*(4), 159–170.

Ribbink, D., van Riel, A. C. R., Liljander, V., & Streukens, S. (2004). Comfort your online customer: Quality, trust and loyalty on the Internet. *Managing Service Quality 14*(6), 446–644.

Roels, G., Karmarkar, U. S., & Carr, S. (2010). Contracting for collaborative services. *Management Science 56*(5), 849–863.

Rousseau, D., Sitkin, M., Burt, R., & Camerer, C. (1998). Not so different after all: A cross-discipline view of trust. *Academy of Management Review 23*(3), 393–404.

Rowley, J. (2006). An analysis of the e-service literature: Towards a research agenda. *Internet Research 16*(3), 339–359.

Rust, R. T., & Chung, T. S. (2006). Marketing models of service and relationships. *Marketing Science 25*(6), 560–580.

Rust, R. T., & Kannan, P. K. (2003). E-service: A new paradigm for business in the electronic environment. *Communications of the ACM 46*(6), 37–44.

Rust, R. T., & Miu, C. (2006). What academic research tells us about service. *Communications of the ACM 49*(7), 49–54.

Savoy, J., & Dolamic, L. (2009). How effective is google's translation service in search? *Communications of the ACM 52*(10), 139–143.

Schmenner, R. W. (2004). Service businesses and productivity. *Decision Sciences 35*(3), 333–347.

Scupola, A. (2008). E-services: Definition, characteristics and taxonomy. *Journal of Electronic Commerce in Organizations 6*(2), 1–4.

Shao, C. Y., Baker, J. A., & Wagner, J. (2004). The effects of appropriateness of service contact personnel dress on customer expectations of service quality and purchase intention: The moderating influences of involvement and gender. *Journal of Business Research 57*, 1164–1176.

Shen, C.-C., & Liao, J.-T. (2007). A study of the relationship among tourism experience, brand image and loyalty—A case study of Janfusun Prince hotel. *Annals of Leisure and Recreation Research 1*(1), 41–70.

Skaanning, C. (2005). *The costs and benefits of customer self-service.* Retrieved February 1, 2011, from website of The Wise Marketer: http://www.thewisemarketer.com/features/read.asp?id=83

Song, H. (2003). E-services at FedEx. *Communications of The ACM 46*(6), 45–46.

Song, L., Song, M., & Benedtto, C. A. (2009). A staged service innovation model. *Decision Sciences 40*(3), 571–599.

Sousa, R., & Voss, C. A. (2009). The effects of service failures and recovery on customer loyalty in e-services: An empirical investigation. *International Journal of Operations & Production Management 29*(8), 834–864.

Spohrer, J., & Maglio, P. P. (2008). The emergence of service science: Toward systematic service innovations to accelerate co-creation of value. *Production and Operations Management 17*(3), 238–246.

Sterman, J. D. (2000). *Business dynamics, systems thinking and modelling for a complex world.* US: McGraw-Hill.

Strate, R. W., & Rappole, C. L. (1997). Strategic alliances between hotels and restaurants. *Journal of Cornell Hospitality Quarterly 38*(3), 50–61. doi:10.1177/001088049703800316

Thaler, R. (1985). Mental accounting and consumer choice. *Marketing Science 4*(Summer), 199–214.

Tiwana, A., & Ramesh, B. (2001). *E-services: Problems, opportunities, and digital platforms.* Symposium conducted at the meeting of System Sciences of Hawaii.

Tung, W. F., & Yuan, S. T. (2008). A service design framework for value co-production: Insight from mutualism perspective. *Kybernetes 37*(2), 226–240.

Tung, W. F., & Yuan, S. T. (2010). Intelligent service machine. *Communications of the ACM 53*(8), 129–134.

ul-Haq, R., & Howcroft, B. (2006). An examination of strategic alliances and the origins of international banking in Europe. *Journal of Service Industry Management 18*(2), 120–139. doi:10.1108/09564230710737781

Ulrich, P. V., Anderson-Connell, L. J., & Wu, W. (2003). Consumer co-design of apparel for mass customization. *Journal of Fashion Marketing and Management 7*(4), 398–412.

Venkatesan, S., Chellappan, C., & Dhavachelvan, P. (2010). Performance analysis of mobile agent failure recovery in e-service applications. *Computer Standards & Interfaces 32*(1–2), 38–43.

Wolfinbarger, M., & Gilly, M. (2003). E-TailQ: Dimensionalizing, measuring and predicting etail quality. *Journal of Retailing 27*, 183–198.

Wu, A. (2011). *Bank of America website down, leaving customers unhappy*, Retrieved February 1, 2011, from website of Epoch Times: http://www.theepochtimes.com/n2/content/view/49326/

Wu, P. C. S., Yeh, G. Y.-Y., & Hsiao, C.-R. (2011). The effect of store image and service quality on brand image and purchase intention for private label brands. *Australiasian Marketing Journal 19*, 30–39.

Zeithaml, V. A. (1988). Consumer perceptions of price, quality, and value: A means-end model and synthesis of evidence. *The Journal of marketing 52*(3), 2–22.

Zeithaml, V. A., Parasuraman, A., & Malhotra, A. (2000). *E-service quality: Definition, dimensions and conceptual model.* Cambridge, MA: Working Paper Marketing Science Institute.

Zeithaml, V. A., Parasuraman, A., & Malhotra, A. (2002). Service quality delivery through web sites: A critical review of extant knowledge. *Journal of the Academy of Marketing Science 30*(4), 362–375.

Zomerdijk, L. G., & Voss, C. A. (2010). Service design for experience-centric services. *Journal of Service Research 13*(1), 67–82.

Index

OTHER TITLES IN QUANTITATIVE APPROACHES TO DECISION MAKING COLLECTION

Donald Stengel, California State University, Fresno, Editor

- *Working With Sample Data: Exploration and Inference* by Priscilla Chaffe-Stengel and Donald N. Stengel
- *Business Applications of Multiple Regression* by Ronny Richardson
- *Operations Methods: Waiting Line Applications* by Ken Shaw
- *Regression Analysis: Understanding and Building Business and Economic Models Using Excel* by J. Holton Wilson, Barry P. Keating and Mary Beal-Hodges
- *Forecasting Across the Organization* by Ozgun Caliskan Demirag, Diane Parente and Carol L. Putman

FORTHCOMING IN THIS COLLECTION

- *Effective Applications of Statistical Process Control 4/15/2014* by Ken Shaw
- *Leveraging Business Analysis for Project Success 5/15/2014* by Vicki James
- *Construction Projects and the Power of Design-Build: Ensuring Safety and Control in Project Delivery using the SAFEDB Methodology 6/15/2014* by Sherif Hashem
- *Project Risk: Concepts, Process, and Tools 7/15/2014* by Tom R. Wielicki and Donald N. Stengel
- *Effective Applications of Supply Chain Logistics 7/15/2014* by Ken Shaw

Announcing the Business Expert Press Digital Library

*Concise E-books Business Students Need
for Classroom and Research*

This book can also be purchased in an e-book collection by your library as
- a one-time purchase,
- that is owned forever,
- allows for simultaneous readers,
- has no restrictions on printing, and
- can be downloaded as PDFs from within the library community.

Our digital library collections are a great solution to beat the rising cost of textbooks. e-books can be loaded into their course management systems or onto student's e-book readers.

The **Business Expert Press** digital libraries are very affordable, with no obligation to buy in future years. For more information, please visit **www.businessexpertpress.com/librarians**. To set up a trial in the United States, please contact **Adam Chesler** at *adam.chesler@ businessexpertpress.com* for all other regions, contact **Nicole Lee** at *nicole.lee@igroupnet.com*.

www.ingramcontent.com/pod-product-compliance
Lightning Source LLC
Chambersburg PA
CBHW070928270326
41927CB00011B/2762